SOUTH SEA ISLANDERS
IN QUEENSLAND

Paul Dillon

Connor Court Publishing

Published in 2024 by Connor Court Publishing
PO Box 7257
Redland Bay, 4165

© Paul Anthony Dillon, 2024

No part of this book may be reproduced in any written, electronic, recording, or photocopying without the written permission of the publisher or author. The exception would be in brief quotations embodied in the critical articles or reviews and pages where permission is specifically granted by the publisher or author.

Although every precaution has been taken to verify the accuracy of the information contained herein, the author and publisher assume no responsibility for any errors or omissions. No liability is assumed for damages that may result from the use of information contained within.

ISBN: 9781923224506

Front Cover image: South Sea islanders by the Fearless; nla.obj-136808052-1.

Design and Typeset by Maria Giordano

Tags: Queensland Colonial history, social and political history of 19th century Queensland; Admiralty, Navigation, Maritime history; Coastal and Island shipping, Sugar Plantations, labour laws, Pacific Islands, Colonisation, Royal Navy, Australian Station, South Sea Islanders, Melanesian and 19th century white trader/South Sea Islander conflict.

Printed in Australia

ABOUT THE AUTHOR

Paul Dillon is a Sunshine Coast based author of Frederick Walker Commandant of the Native Police, Connor Court Publishing, Brisbane 2018;

The Murder of John Francis Dowling and the Massacre of 300 Aborigines, Connor Court Publishing, Brisbane 2019;

Inside the Killing Fields Hornet Bank, Cullin-la-Ringo & The Maria Wreck, Connor Court Publishing, Brisbane 2020;

Queensland Native Police, The First Twenty Years, 2020;

The Irvinebank Massacre, Connor Court Publishing, Brisbane 2021;

Fraser Island Massacre Vrai ou Faux, Connor Court Publishing, Brisbane 2022;

Bêche-de-mer and the Binghis, 2022;

The History of Bêche-de-mer Fishing in Queensland Waters and Adjacent Islands, Connor Court Publishing, Brisbane 2023;

Dispela Kantri Bilong Mi, Nau! Queensland Annexes New Guinea, 2023;

Kanaka Boats is A-Comin' Pacific Island Labourers in Queensland, 2023;

Queensland's contribution to the development of British New Guinea, Connor Court Publishing, Brisbane 2023;

The Queensland Native Police, The Final Years, 2024.

He holds a Bachelor of Arts degree from the Australian National University. Paul joined the Commonwealth Public Service in 1965. On 23 May 1986, he was called to the Bar of New South Wales and practised as a barrister in the Criminal Division of the superior courts of Queensland as counsel for the defence.

THE RECENT SOUTH SEA MASSACRE.—TERRIBLE SCENES ON BOARD THE "YOUNG DICK."

Illustrated News 15 July 1886 p 16

Contents

Foreword by Geoffrey Blainey — 9

Introduction — 11

Chapter 1 — 21

Chapter 2 — 133

Chapter 3 — 157

Chapter 4 — 182

Table A Marine Incidents — 202

Number of Labour Vessel Trips per Year & Passengers Queensland — 213

Bibliography — 214

SOUTH SEA ISLANDS

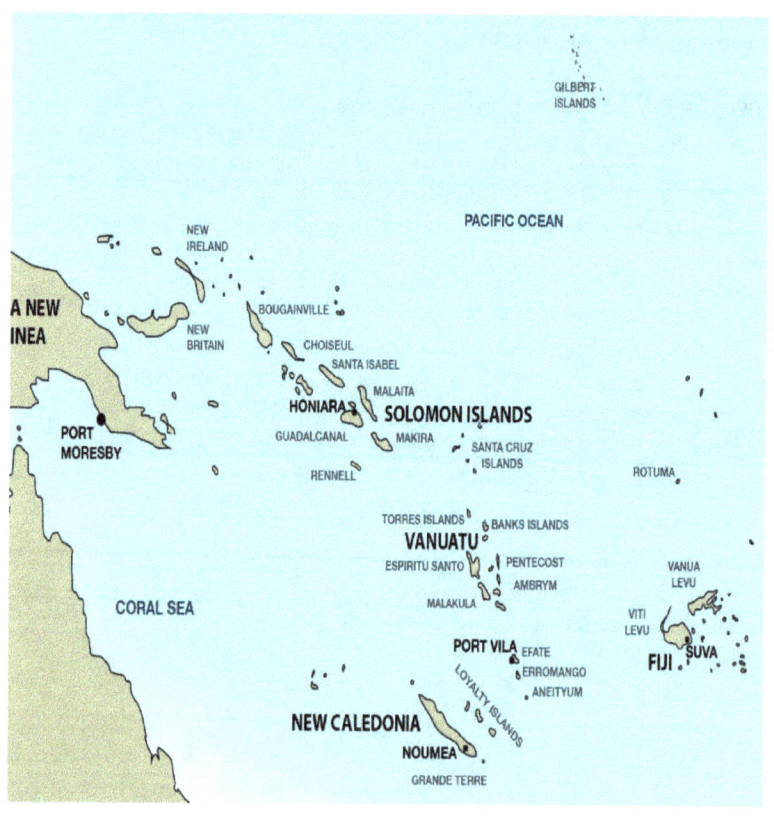

Foreword

Geoffrey Blainey

South Sea Islanders in Queensland is one of the most controversial topics studied by Australian historians. It is entangled with the sister topic of racism. It is complicated because it involves labourers shipped to Australia, in the course of half a century, from some 80 different Pacific Islands. Here also is a vital strand in our nation's political history, for it led to one of the few secession campaigns: the hope in the 1880s that coastal north Queensland would break away from Brisbane and form a seventh colony or state.

Almost everywhere in the world in the 19th century, sugar cane was a stronghold of coloured labour: the belief was universal that white men could not perform outdoors manual work in a very hot climate. As more and more sugar was produced in Australia, the heart of the sugar industry moved to the tropical coast of Queensland. To find the necessary labourers, ships visited an array of South West Pacific islands including New Guinea, Vanuatu and the Solomons. The recruiting was often brutal but often peaceful. If you read about this traffic and trade in such easily-found sources as Wikipedia and Encyclopedia Britannica, and then turn to Paul Dillon's latest book, you will sometimes wonder whether you are reading about the same episode in history.

Dillon often sets out long documents which give readers an

opportunity to learn more and more, and even to make up their mind. Thus, he challenges the prevailing view that these islanders were usually shipped home like sheep without any worthwhile gain. And yet here, without much comment, is a brief aside on a return voyage from Queensland in the ship *Spunkie*. Scores of the islanders had crammed into the ship's hold a small mountain of luggage "some of them having as many as three and four large boxes of clothes, besides loose articles of furniture and cooking utensils. The boxes, in addition to clothes and drapery of all descriptions, contained carpenters' tools, such as adzes, tomahawks, chisels, gimblets, hand-saws, butchers' knives; rifles, double-barrelled guns, ammunition."

Since 2018, as a fulltime researcher living on the Sunshine Coast, Dillon has written book after book. At present there is probably no researcher in an Australian university who can equal his knowledge on this vital set of topics. One reason for his success is that he has not only resurrected a collection of key witnesses – islanders themselves, sugar-cane growers, missionaries, sea captains, British naval officers, and politicians – but also cross-examined them with a barrister's skill.

Introduction

In my book *Bêche-de-mer and the Binghis*, I explained how I hit on the idea of writing about marine incidents in Queensland waters that involved indigenes. When I came to examine the maritime history of colonial Queensland, 1859 to Federation, I found that the colony of Queensland had involved itself in more than one indigenous group of people. The obvious group would be the natives who were the descendants of the original inhabitants of Australia, Aboriginals. But, after examining the record, I found the colony of Queensland had dealings with or control of not only Aboriginals but Torres Strait Islanders, Papuans and Pacific Islanders. So, the project had to be extended. That has resulted in three books. The first in the series is *Bêche-de-mer and the Binghis* dealing with native-born Australian Aboriginals and Torres Strait Islanders. The second book is *Dispela Kantri Belong Mi, Nau!* dealing with indigenous Papuans. The final book relates to marine incidents under the jurisdiction of the colony of Queensland involving indigenous Pacific Islanders also known as South Sea Islanders.[1]

---

1   This book is an abridged edition of *Kanaka Boats is A-Comin' Pacific Island Labourers in Queensland* by Paul Dillon, 2023

For the sake of clarity, I define a marine incident as follows:

> The death of or injury to officers and/or crew and/or passengers of a vessel.
>
> The loss of or damage to a vessel and/or the cargo; and/or
>
> A breach of Admiralty or Maritime legislation.[2]

In opening the first Parliament of Queensland on 29 May 1860, the Governor said, among other things:

> Along our sea-coast and on the banks of our rivers, we possess millions of acres which bear the same relation to the cotton and sugar, which the great pastoral districts of the interior hold to the wool manufactures of the mother country. Next to a wise management of the public lands, a good system of immigration is, perhaps, the most essential element in the prosperity of a new country. Provision has been made by the Government, under the regulations now in force, for a supply of labour from the mother country, adequate to the requirements of the present year.[3]

A Select Committee of the Legislative Assembly, appointed on 31 May 1860, to consider and report on the best means of promoting immigration to the Colony of Queensland made the following recommendation among others:

> The question as to the propriety of introducing into this colony Indian Coolies, Chinese, or the ordinary class of German immigrants, is not favourably entertained by the witnesses, generally; your Committee would not, therefore, recommend that any such immigration should be carried on in any way at the cost of the Government; but, at the same time, consider that no restriction should be thrown in the way of parties desirous

---

2 See the Australian Maritime Safety Authority for a comprehensive definition of a marine incident.

3 Moreton Bay Courier 31 May 1860 p 2.

of procuring such a description of labour at their own cost, and under the proper supervision of the Government.⁴

On 20 November 1862, the Duke of Newcastle advised Governor Bowen:

> ... to inform the petitioners who are opposed to the employment of Asiatic labour in the colony, that no sufficient grounds are shown for depriving Queensland of a supply of Indian labour if the community at large desires to have it; that the local Legislature is the only constitutional exponent of the will of the community; and that the Legislature, having passed an Act clearly sanctioning the measure, has violated no constitutional principle by leaving the details to the discretion of the Executive Government.⁵

A great press controversy arose in Brisbane over Mr. R. Towns's cotton plantation on the Logan River. As a consequence, he wrote to the R. G. W. Herbert, Colonial Secretary of Queensland.

> I came to the conclusion that cotton growing upon a large scale either must be abandoned in Queensland, or be carried out by cheaper labour. It will be in your recollection that the legislature took the necessary steps to encourage Coolie labour from India;⁶ availing of this, I despatched a ship to Madras and Calcutta, to carry it out, but the scheme failed from the unwillingness of the Indian government to extend the facilities for drawing away the labour from the vast public works now being carried on in that Empire,—such at least was alleged as the reason, though, possibly, jealousy of our entering the lists as competitors with them in cotton growing was not without, its influence.

---

4   Moreton Bay Courier 6 Sep 1860 p 4.
5   GG VOL. IV.] 28 January 1863 [No. 8 p 69.
6   See Courier 17 July 1862 p 6, for a discussion on The Attempt to Introduce Indian Labour; see also QSA ID ITM1098209 Mr R Towns requesting the Government to introduce Chinese labourers.

> Baffled by the proposed Indian Coolie Immigration, I turned my attention to the South Sea Islanders. I have for many years been engaged in trade amongst these so-called "savages," and have had many hundreds of them in my employ, both onshore and onboard ship, and found them an industrious, tractable, and inoffensive race. For the greater part of the work on a cotton plantation, I believe these islanders will be found well-suited. The question of any species of slavery or kidnapping of these natives is at once confuted by the instructions to the captain of the vessel and the interpreter, and my letter to the missionaries, which I append hereto.[7] The men thoroughly understand the nature of their contract, both as to their treatment and wages here and as to my returning them to their own country when their time (which you will observe is only for one year) shall have expired. It is my intention to persevere in the attempt to grow cotton with this kind of labour, on short agreements; and if the men like the work and country, to try to persuade them to bring their wives with them. R. Towns. Sydney, August 31, 1863.[8]

Cotton was grown principally in the Ipswich district, although there were many other localities in which it was cultivated successfully. However, many planters abandoned cotton for sugar as a more profitable crop; perhaps, because of the end of the American Civil War, with American cotton again entering the world market. In 1869, 14,426 acres were under cotton, with 1,118,899 lbs. exported for the year.[9] In 1870, 6,341 acres of land were under cultivation with sugar cane. This was an increase of 1,176 acres of sugar cane over 1869.[10] During the year 1868, after the act for regulating Polynesian immigration came into force, six vessels arrived from the South Sea Islands, bringing 437 males and 2 females. In 1869, five ships arrived, with 276

---

7 Courier 2 September 1863 p 2, published Towns's instructions to his labour recruiters.
8 Courier 8 September 1863 p 2, abridged; see the full letter at pp 26-29 below.
9 Statistics of Queensland 1869 pp 154-155. Pugh's Almanac and Directory for 1872 p 332.
10 Statistics of Queensland 1870 pp 130-131.

males and 2 females. In 1870, nine ships arrived, with 581 males and 14 females.[11]

A largely attended public meeting was held at the School of Arts on 8 March 1869, to pass resolutions condemnatory of the introduction of Polynesians into Queensland. The Rev. W. Woolcock moved as follows:

> This meeting is of the opinion that the Polynesian Labourers' Act of 1868 (31 Vic, No. 47) now in operation, has failed to accomplish the object for which it was ostensibly passed, viz.: For the prevention of abuses, for the regulation of the traffic, and for securing to the labourers proper treatment and protection; that it exercises no control nor supervision over the traffic in the islands, fosters kidnapping, and affords facilities for the commission of other crimes with comparative impunity, while it is powerless to prevent deception and fraud, both in the manner of obtaining the natives and in the agreements alleged to be entered into with them, and provides no security for insuring their return to their respective homes. That in the opinion of this meeting, any further attempt to legislate upon this subject will be perfectly useless and unproductive of any good results; inasmuch as it is beyond the power of the Parliament of Queensland, as a subordinate legislature to pass—or of the Government to carry out—any Act which will prevent the abuses to which this system is liable, and which have already become as notorious as they are disgraceful. The system of Polynesian labour in force in Queensland was incipient slavery, and if it was not slavery now, it was likely to become so.[12]

In the House of Commons on 28 June 1869, Mr. Taylor asked the Under-Secretary of State for the Colonies whether his attention had been called to the great dissatisfaction prevailing in Queensland over the system of importation of South Sea Islanders; whether he was aware that this system was described as

---

11 Pugh's Almanac and Directory for 1872 p 120.
12 Brisbane Courier 9 March 1869 p 3, abridged.

practically no better than a legalised slave trade that the natives were in many cases inveigled on board under false pretences, or kidnapped by force and whether he would lay on the table any correspondence on the subject.

> Mr. Adderley said there was a confusion in the statements which had been made between the kidnapping of the South Sea Islanders for service in the Fiji Islands, and the regular immigration of South Sea Islanders into Queensland, for the purpose of cotton cultivation. The outrages committed were in connection with the former, and he knew of no means of checking the system. As to the immigration into Queensland, he believed it was properly conducted, for the Queensland Legislature had passed regulations stricter even than those made by the Imperial and the Indian Governments for the protection of the coolies sent to the West Indies. It was unfair, therefore, to the colonists to make these high-coloured and unfounded statements; and nothing could be more injurious both to the colonists and the South Sea Islanders themselves than to raise a general cry against the slave trade, and under cover of it, to stop legitimate immigration. This immigration was carried on with a civilised country where the natives could be made use of for labour and might become civilised by their contact with a civilised race. This was a matter to be dealt with by the Queensland Legislature alone. It was true that if there was a revival of the slave trade in any form, this would be a matter of Imperial policy, but there was no shadow of proof that this was a revival of the slave trade.[13]

The plantations of Mr. G. Raff (late of the Caboolture Sugar Company), and Captain Whish, were situated on Caboolture Creek.[14] About six miles from Mackay were the principal sugar plantations, viz.: the Alexandra, belonging to Davidson and Co., having 240 acres under cane; Mr. Spiller's, on the north bank of the river, having about 60 acres; whilst between the plantations

---

13 Sydney Morning Herald 2 September 1869 p 2.
14 Pugh's Almanac and Directory for 1863 p 161.

of Messrs. Lloyd and Holmes there were, at the end of 1867, about 80 or 100 acres more.[15]

The sugar cane industry was labour-intensive, both in terms of skilled and unskilled work. Fields had to be cleared and burned with the remaining ash then used as a fertiliser. Sometimes land had to be terraced, and irrigation networks built and kept clear. A great number of planters and harvesters were required to plant, weed, and cut the cane which was ready for harvest five or six months after planting in the most fertile areas. Harvesting was a more intense period requiring labourers to work night and day. Carts had to be loaded and oxen tended to take the cane to the processing plant. The sugar then had to be packed and transported to ports for shipping. All the above tasks were done by island labourers.

QSA ITM1683485 DR22994

The manner of South Sea Islander recruiting might be described as follows:

---
15 Pugh's Almanac and Directory for 1863 p 201.

About £2000 was required—and very often several people clubbed together to raise it, and buy an old sailing vessel, a schooner. The craft was then painted and fitted out according to the government regulations for the trade. She was then surveyed by the Government surveyor, and on his favourable report the vessel was granted a licence to carry so many boys, as the islanders were called, and so many Marys, as the women were called. The vessel, when provisioned and made ready for the voyage, shipped a white crew and a government agent, which she was compelled to do by law. On the way to the South Seas, the vessel stopped at one of the nearest islands so that boat crews could be obtained, such as the Island of Tanna, where they were experts in boats in all weathers. These boat crews were a very hardy and obedient race of men, and they were good shots as well as good sailors; it would not be easy to do without such support to a labour vessel. The native crews were returned to their home islands after the recruiting was completed. The vessel then began a cruise among the islands, looking out for recruits. In many islands, it was customary to light a smoke fire as a signal that the islanders wanted to trade. Two boats would then go ashore, rowed by the native boat crew carrying a white man, who was known as the 'recruiter' and the government agent. One of these boats had on board the trade by which the recruiting was effected. This boat went ashore; while the second boat, which was called the cover boat, kept a short distance outside the surf to cover the retreat of the trading boat if it became necessary. When the first boat approached the shore, the bargaining was conducted in the following manner: There was a headman on the beach, with several assistants belonging to him. They kept the boys and the Marys in the background while the headman made the bargain. Only one boy was bought and sold at a time. The headman, who gets into the trade boat, begins to bargain with the recruiter for the boy, and on their agreeing upon the price, the trade was taken from the trade chest and passed to the headman at the same moment the boy was passed into the boat. To make the thing legal, the men or women were taken on board before the government agent and the captain, and the question asked, through an interpreter, whether they would like to go to

Queensland and work for three years. If the boy consented to go to Queensland, his reply was duly entered on the ship's log or the government agent's official book. The following was an average price given for a boy: One Snider rifle or two muskets, two dozen pipes, fifty sticks of negro-head tobacco, ten boxes of matches, five fathoms of calico, one fathom of Turkey, red calico, one American axe, one tomahawk, three sheath knives, and about twenty rounds of ammunition. For such a boy, the vessel received on landing in Australia £20, and the number of boys the vessel was allowed to carry was about 110 to every 100 tons of the ship's register. For every Mary — the captain and owners receive the sum of £10. As the vessel averages a little over 100 tons, 130 to 150 boys and Marys may be regarded as an average full cargo. The trade was a paying one to all concerned.[16]

In my above two books, I outlined the parameters of the study of indigenous contact with Queensland maritime traffic during the colonial period of Queensland history, 1859 to Federation. The study is limited to marine incidents involving an indigenous element. As I pointed out above, Queensland during its colonial period engaged or administered four broad groups of indigenous

---

16 Age 27 December 1884 p 13. The South Sea islanders and the Queensland labour trade, a record of voyages and experiences in the western Pacific, from 1875 to 1891 by Wawn, William T; Hay, William Delisle 1893 London: S. Sonnenschein & co pp 3-4, 8-11.

peoples: Aboriginals and Torres Strait Islanders, Papuans, and South Sea Islanders. These groups had one factor in common, they were *indigènes non civilisés* and never really formed part of the colonial fabric of Queensland society. Attempts were made to conduct civil and humane intercourse with these groups. The Imperial government, the Queensland government, missionaries, and Exeter Hall groups all spent a good deal of time and money in endeavouring to treat and elevate these *indigènes non civilisés* to what was at the time considered an acceptable standard of living, perhaps analogous to the standard of a white man.

In 1994, the Commonwealth Government formally recognised Australian South Sea Islanders as a distinct community and in 2000 the Queensland Government followed suit. That government also recognised the discrimination, injustice, disadvantage and prejudice experienced by Australian South Sea Islanders throughout history and the significant disadvantage the community still faces today.[17]

---

17 https://humanrights.gov.au/our-work/race- discrimination/publications/australian-south-sea-islanders-century-race#45

1

Colonial Use of Kanaka Labour

A Pacific Islander was defined in the Polynesian Labourers' Act of 1868, as a Polynesian labourer from the South Sea Islands, or a South Sea Islander;[18] also known as a kanaka from the vernacular. The ethnic or racial category of these individuals is Melanesian.

There is no need for me to define the South Sea Islands. In the vernacular of the day, it was a common term of usage and fully comprehended by the citizens of the colonies of New South Wales, Tasmania, Victoria and Queensland. In shipping circles, it was a regular destination for ships clearing Port Jackson. For the year ending 1857, 18 ships under British colours entered the colony of New South Wales together with 10 foreign ships from the South Sea Islands, a total tonnage of 3,437.[19] The London Missionary Society operated out of Sydney and their ship the *John Williams* regularly sailed from Sydney to their mission stations in the South Sea Islands, while their Sydney-based pastors regularly gave talks on their missionary activities in the islands.

The *Velocity* sailed for the islands on 31 January 1847 to recruit native labourers for Messrs. Boyd and Co., New South Wales. In

---

18 31° VICTORIÆ No. 47. Supplement to the Queensland Government Gazette of Saturday, 29 February 1868, No. 30 p 217.

19 Empire 24 February 1858 p 5.

this mission, Captain Kirsopp was very successful; he obtained sixty-five strong able-bodied men, twenty-six from the island of Tanna, twenty-three from Lifou, and sixteen from Aneityum. Sixty-two of these were landed at Boyd Town, for Maneroo,[20] to be employed as shepherds, and the other three were brought to Sydney, as a specimen of the kind of men available.[21]

The *Australian* of 4 May 1847, published a lengthy editorial on Mr. Boyd importing coloured labour into New South Wales:

> Did we desire to exhibit, in the most glowing colours, the deplorable barrenness of the labour market of New South Wales, we think we could hit upon no expedient so startlingly demonstrative as the recent appalling cannibal importation to which we have been subjected. It is a fearful picture of the frightful alternative to which want and difficulty, will induce stock-holders to have recourse — an alternative daring, dangerous, and disgusting — one against which the universal voice should be upraised — against which the Government should be alert to watch and ward us. Averse, on principle, to the Coolie labour of India, more than sceptical as to the coveted importation of Pagan Chinese or the ruthless introduction of sanguinary Malays — still, the debarkation of merciless hordes of man-eating savages was a consummation of horror too revolting to enter our dull conceptions. The deed, however, has been done — an advanced guard of sixty-five bloodsuckers has already polluted our shores, and unless we be up and doing, we may behold these tractable lambs, like wolves in sheep's clothing, pour in upon us, drove by drove, to devour the flocks they are designed to protect.[22]

About a year later, the *Australian* was again up in arms over Mr. Boyd's South Sea Islanders. They ran an article in which

---

20 Now known as Monaro, New South Wales.
21 Sydney Morning Herald 21 April 1847 p 2.
22 Australian 4 May 1847 p 3, abridged.

they accused Captain Marceau and the Jesuit Missionaries of kidnapping about thirty of the South Sea Islanders who, for the last ten or twelve months, had been in the service of Mr. Boyd. By various arts and with the aid of a plentiful supply of coconuts, they were kidnapped by a company of Jesuits and brought onboard the French ship, *Arche d'Alliance* which suddenly sailed on Good Friday, 21 April 1848. Mr. Boyd, through Mr. J. P. Robinson, requested Archbishop Polding to intervene, but Dr. Polding declined as he had no control over the French Mission. Mr. Robinson thereupon obtained from the magistrate of the Water Police warrants for the apprehension of the men but the ship sailed before the warrants could be executed.[23]

It was subsequently reported in the *Sydney Chronicle* that Captain Marceau took seventeen natives back to their homes and families, and was obliged, from want of space, to refuse a passage to many of their companions who earnestly implored it.[24]

The *Scotia*, which arrived from the South Sea Islands, brought intelligence of the death of Captain Blake, who was murdered by the natives of the island of Eddisrone.[25] Mr. Sutton, the chief officer, brought the vessel to Sydney and reported that Captain Blake and a boat's crew went on shore on 20 May 1858, for trading, when Blake was struck on the neck and head in three places with a tomahawk, and two of the crew were severely wounded. Fortunately, the crew succeeded in getting the boat onboard the schooner. Captain Blake lingered for five days, then died, the others, providentially, recovered. No reason can be assigned for the perpetration of this atrocious deed, as they

---

23 Australian 28 April 1848 p 2, abridged.
24 Sydney Chronicle 9 May 1848 p 3.
25 Most likely the island of Eddystone (Simbo), Solomons Islands.

appeared to be quite friendly up to the moment of the attack.[26]

H.M.S. Iris returned to Sydney on 6 September 1858, after settling accounts with some of the South Sea Islanders. Captain Loring burnt the villages and plantations of the natives at Tanna and Woodlark Islands, giving them distinctly to understand that it was in punishment for the murder of Captain Outtrim at the former place, and of the crew of the *Gazelle* at the latter. Mr. Tupper, a mate on board the *Iris*, and Kennedy, first-class petty officer, were killed by the natives at Tanna, owing to their being cut off from the rest of the shore party in the attack. Kennedy's body was not recovered, but that of Mr. Tupper was carried on board, and buried at sea. This young man had passed his examination and was about to join the *Shannon* as a lieutenant.[27]

Messrs. James Paddon and Co.,[28] of Noumea, financed a commercial venture for sandalwood, bêche-de-mer & tortoiseshell along the north coast of Queensland. In June 1860, the brig *Julia Percy*, W. Banner, master, left Port de France (Noumea), and, after calling at various islands of the Loyalty and New Hebrides Groups, to obtain natives, pigs, and yams, took her final departure from Erromango for Lizard Island, on the north-east coast of Australia, on July 16. Of the seventy-six persons on board, seventeen were white men, seven Chinese, and two half-caste children, while the remainder were natives of the Solomon Islands, New Caledonia, Nengone or Mare, Drehu or Lifou, Tanna, Aneityum, and Erromango.[29]

The reader might ask what was the need for the importing of islander labourers. A Mr George Poole writing under the nom de plume of Quidam circulated a lengthy pamphlet on the need

---

26 Moreton Bay Courier 21 July 1858 p 2.
27 Moreton Bay Courier 15 September 1858 p 2.
28 https://www.isfar.org.au/bio/paddon-james-1811-1861/
29 Sydney Morning Herald 6 January 1862 p 4.

for labour in Moreton Bay and the neighbouring district. He said,

> On account of the scarcity of labour. That the demand for labour has vastly exceeded the supply is so well known that no arguments are needed to prove it. All parties admit the fact. If our labour demand is not supplied, we shall have Chinese, South Sea Islanders, and suchlike Pagans supplied in their stead, which species of labour is of a far worse description, attended with evils of the most frightful kind. The South Sea Islanders are cannibals, devourers of human flesh, pagans and addicted to the practice of enormities at which the very blood of a civilised being runs cold. If savages of these classes are imported to supply the labour market, their importation will speedily lapse into slavery; and as it is, those already brought here are dealt with as so many marketable cattle. They are bought, sold, exchanged—a traffic made with them, and dealt with literally as so many slaves.

R. Towns & Co, in 1854, took steps to secure a foothold in Brisbane when the company bought the Commercial Hotel, Wharf, and Store in South Brisbane from Mr. McCabe for £3000.[30]

The schooner *Don Juan*, arrived in Brisbane on 17 August 1863, from the New Hebrides. She brought a number of the natives of those islands to be employed as labourers by Captain Towns on his cotton plantation, on the Logan River, at the rate of 10s. per month, with rations. There were sixty-seven natives on board, one man died on the passage.[31]

---

30 Sydney Morning Herald 14 February 1854 p 5.
31 Courier 18 Aug 1863 p 5. See also QSA ID ITM1238614 Health Officer's Report on the passengers of the labour ship *Don Juan*.

The presence of these natives in Brisbane caused Mr. Theophilus Pugh M.L.A., to ask the Colonial Secretary whether the South Sea Islanders lately arrived in the *Don Juan* had been kidnapped in the manner adopted by the Peruvian vessels. The Colonial Secretary said he had inquired into the matter, and had been informed that they had come under distinctly signed contracts to work for one year, and then to be returned whence they came.[32]

The *North Australian and Queensland General Advertiser* of 20 August 1863, published a commentary under the heading, *The Slave Trade In Queensland*, arising out of the *Don Juan* bringing in contracted native labourers; and noted, "it is a crying disgrace upon the colony, and can only bring a curse with it; no reason can be urged for such an unnatural proceeding when hundreds of thousands of our fellow countrymen are starving at home, seeking employment and cannot find it."[33]

DON JUAN — SLAVE TRADE IN QUEENSLAND.

(To the Editor of the *Courier*.)

> Under the above heading, I find a paragraph in the *North Australian*, in which the writer is pleased to indulge in some remarks relative to Captain Towns' recent importation of South Sea Islanders. A copy of Captain Towns' instructions to the master of the vessel and the interpreter, also his letter to the missionaries, and the form of agreement with the natives, I have handed to the Hon. the Colonial Secretary, who, in reply to the questions of Theophilus P. Pugh, Esq., M.L.A., has laid them on the table of the house.
>
> I would just take notice of the concluding portion of the paragraph under review—about it being a crying disgrace &c., &c., &c. I can only say that I believe such men as Captain Towns

---

32 Courier 19 Aug 1863 p 3.

33 North Australian and Queensland General Advertiser 20 August 1863 p 3.

are likely to be of more use to the "starving thousands" at home than the editor of the *North Australian* and Theophilus P. Pugh, Esq., M.L.A. I think his offer to bring fifty Lancashire families out at his own expense, and his munificent donation to the Relief Fund (which may still be in the recollection of some of your readers) may be considered sufficient evidence that he is as mindful of the necessities of the poor people at home as all these pseudo patriots.

In conclusion, I would say that the law of Queensland, as it at present stands, enables any capitalist to import and employ what labour he pleases. How will Captain Towns be deterred from getting as many of these Islanders as he likes, though he incurs the risk of the heavy displeasure of Theophilus P. Pugh, Esq., M.L.A., and the thunders of the *North Australian*.

So anxious were these natives to come, when the matter was properly explained to them, that the captain had literally to drive about 100 of them on shore again. Proper huts for them, and a large room to mess in, have been erected on the plantation; and if Theophilus P. Pugh, Esq., M.L.A., wants to prevent the importation of these people, let him bring in a bill, and see if he can get it carried. Yours obediently, W. H. Palmer. South Brisbane, August 22.[34]

Mr. Pugh, M.L.A. requested the Queensland government to table the correspondence relating to the *Don Juan*, which was done and published in the *Courier* of 2 September 1863.[35]

The following letter to the Colonial Secretary from Mr. R. Towns sets out his reasons for importing South Sea Islanders to work on his cotton plantation:

> My attention has been called to the report of certain proceedings in the Assembly, in reference to the introduction of a number of natives from the South Sea Islands, by the schooner *Don Juan*, for special services at my cotton plantation on the Logan. The

---

34 Courier 24 August 1863 p 2.
35 Courier 2 September 1863 p 2.

remarks in some of the newspapers to which this matter has given rise, I would, as I usually do, have treated with the silent contempt they merit; but the proceedings in this case, in which you have been called upon in your official place in parliament to answer questions on a subject in which I am alone responsible, seem to me to be out of the ordinary course, and compel me in justice to you, as well as to myself, to state clearly the principle on which I have acted.

It may be in your recollection that at the time when so much anxiety prevailed for the growth of cotton in Queensland with the view to the development of a new industrial resource in the colony, as well as to supply the want of raw material under which, the Lancashire operatives were suffering so much, I applied for, and took up a maximum grant of cotton land—upon this speculation, I have spent upwards of six thousand pounds without, as yet, any return. It is true that the season has been much against the experiment, but the question of labour has had much more to do with this result and has induced me to embark on the present South Sea Island Immigration. Meanwhile, I had engaged the services of a number of Germans, imported under the regulations and at the expense of the colony. These men, led away by the bad advice of their countrymen and others, who, on their arrival, persuaded them that they were working for wages below the current rates, became so discontented that they either bolted or rendered their services almost worse than useless so that my agent was glad to give up all claim to the fellows, whose laziness, combined with their large ration consuming and useless family, (for your laws do not seem to reach the wives and children), would have soon ruined the whole enterprise. Observing that others similarly engaged in the cotton experiment were, like myself, suffering from the effects of European labour, I came to the conclusion that cotton growing on a large scale either must be abandoned in Queensland, or be carried out by cheaper labour. It will be in your recollection that the legislature took the necessary steps to encourage Coolie labour from India; availing of this, I despatched a ship to Madras and Calcutta, to carry it out, but the scheme failed from the unwillingness of the Indian government to extend the facilities for drawing away the labour from the vast public works now being carried on in that Empire,—such at least was alleged as the reason, though, possibly, jealousy of our entering the lists as competitors with them in cotton growing was not without its influence.

Thus, baffled by the proposed Indian Coolie Immigration, I turned my attention to a class of people, to whom I am no stranger—the South Sea Islanders. I have for many years been engaged in trade amongst these so-called "savages," and have had many hundreds of them in my employ, both onshore and onboard ship, and found them an industrious, tractable, and inoffensive race. I have always placed confidence in them, and they have, I believe, the greatest confidence in me and in my fulfilling the engagements I make with them, spending as I do many thousands annually amongst them in their islands.

For the greater part of the work on a cotton plantation, I believe these islanders will be found well suited; and instead of being attacked and branded in the way I have been, I think I deserve the thanks of the community for the introduction of that kind of labour which is suited to our wants, and which may save us from the inhumanity of driving to the exposed labour of fieldwork, the less tropically hardy European women and children, for I suppose the most thorough advocate for European labour will admit, that in cotton clearing and picking, they, as well as the men, must take part in the labour.

Apart from the outburst of angry feeling and the senseless howl with which the *Don Juan's* arrival has been greeted, I feel confident I have the good wishes of the employers of labour by substituting this native labour for the generous (!) pale faces who have been brought out at the expense of the country, who delight in scheming about rather than in honest working, and who feel insulted if you offer them for a day's work that which they have been accustomed to receive at home for a week's labour.

It is these drones in the hive of industry, whom I call the "breeches pocket patriots," who first drove me to the employment of native labour, and it is those men, or others pandering to their feelings and passions, who, after putting the colony to so much expense for their passage and having done little or nothing to repay it, now seek to raise an outcry against those who cost the colony nothing for their passage, and who, I venture to predict, will leave a lasting benefit behind them.

The question of any species of slavery or kidnapping of these natives is at once confuted by the instructions to the captain of the vessel and the interpreter, and my letter to the missionaries, which I append hereto. [The instructions and letter were published in the *Courier* of the 3rd instant.] The men thoroughly understand the nature of their contract, both as to their treatment and wages here and as to my returning them to their own country when their time (which you will observe is only for one year) shall have expired. It is my intention to persevere in the attempt to grow cotton with this kind of labour, on short agreements; and if the men like the work and country, to try to persuade them to bring their wives with them. As to the danger expressed by some of the newspaper's scribblers, lest the government be put to enormous expense in the additional police requisite to keep these "barbarians" in order, I venture to predict that there will be less crime amongst them, if not interfered with by these agitators, than amongst an equal number of European labourers from whatever country they may have been drawn at the public expense. R. Towns. Sydney, August 31, 1863.[36]

On or about September 1864, R. Towns & Co.'s schooner, *Uncle Tom* was towed downriver to Lytton, by the *Premier, s.s.* She was bound for the South Sea Islands, to return the islanders imported in 1863 by Captain R. Towns, to their native places. After landing her passengers, the schooner cruised among the islands in search of bêche-de-mer and then returned to Brisbane with islanders who had entered into an engagement of labour.[37]

---

36 Courier 8 September 1863 p 2. See also QSA ID ITM1098209 Mr R Towns requesting the Government to introduce Chinese labourers.
37 Brisbane Courier 13 September 1864 p 2.

The *Brisbane Courier* of 21 March 1865 ran the following editorial:

> The white labourer not only dies too fast, but he also charges too high. He will have the price of his life, and that price is one which the planter cannot afford to pay. Australia is far worse off on this point than America. She has no such reservoir of white labour near at hand. Her free population reaches her across three oceans in driblets and is speedily absorbed. To cultivate her northern coasts, therefore, acclimatised labourers from intertropical countries will have to be introduced, and probably to a great extent. It is with great satisfaction that we find from the letter of our intelligent correspondent that the absurd clamour which has been raised against the introduction of coloured labour into the colony has almost entirely subsided. A couple of years ago, Captain Towns was morally crucified for having introduced, under special conditions, a cargo of labourers from the islands of Oceania. He was stigmatised as a slave dealer, a second Legree; and the philanthropic colonists were much inclined to look upon every one of his tawny charges as a second Uncle Tom. This nonsense is now at an end. Let us hope, forever. The Queenslanders are only too glad to get tropical labourers, whether Kanakas, Coolies, or Chinese; and there is every prospect of a stream of Oriental immigration setting in which will make Australia as independent of foreign importation for the luxuries of life as she will, if left to her untrammelled energies, certainly become for its necessaries.[38]

At this stage of Queensland's economy, the supply of labour was a critical factor in the development of the only resources available for exploitation for wealth creation, such as bêche-de-mer, sugar, cotton and pastoral pursuits. For instance, sugar growing at Mackay was beginning to assume a very promising appearance and fresh plantations were being laid down. Furthermore, white labour at Mackay was very scarce, and the sugar fields were being cultivated almost entirely by kanakas, who buckled down to their work well. This cheap and tractable supply of labour allowed entrepreneurs to commence and

---

38 Brisbane Courier 21 March 1865 p 3.

carry out operations with relatively small amounts of capital. The table below shows the early stages of sugar production in Queensland.[39]

	1867	1868	1869	1870	1871	1872
No. of Sugar Mills	6	10	28	39	55	65
No. of Sugar Refineries				1	1	1
Total acres of land under crop	31559	39321	47,034	52,210	59,969	62,191
Total acres under Sugar Cane	1,995	3,896	5,165	6,341	9,581	11,757
Total acres of Cane crushed			1,238	2,188	3,078	5,018
Quantity of Sugar made in tons	168	619	1,490	2,854	3,762	6,266

The table below indicates the inflow of kanakas into the colony and their areas of employment.[40]

Date	Place	Ship	Kanakas	Remarks
17/8/1863	Brisbane	Don Juan	67	Cotton plantation
13/10/1866	Bowen	Percy	50	Bêche-de-mer
13/7/1867	Bowen	Fanny Nicholson	201	Shepherds
16/8/1867	Brisbane	King Oscar	222	To squatrs, sugar & cotton
9/11/1867	Maryborough	Mary Smith	84	22 to sugar balance to others
13/5/1867	Mackay	Prima Donna	70	50 to sugar balance to others
1868	Queensland	Labour vessels	604	Total for Sugar
1869	Queensland	Labour vessels	313	Total for Sugar

Moreover, the supply side of the labour market was not regulated. The demand for labour was met by shipowners and others

---

39 Qld V & P of LA 1882 Vol I p 834.

40 The table is sourced from Queensland daily newspapers of the time and QSA IDITM18834.

sending vessels to the various South Sea Islands recruiting natives ad libitum to meet the demand. For example:

> Each boy signs the subjoined agreement with his employer and is thereby brought under the protection of the Masters and Servants Act, 1861, (Qld) so that any pretext for an outcry about slavery is entirely done away with. It is, we believe, Mr. Crossley's intention to proceed to Sydney by the next *Boomerang* for the purpose of chartering a smart schooner capable of carrying 150 Kanakas, and he expects to return with them in from three to four months — that is to say, if he has applications for that number, otherwise he will take them to Maryborough, where one firm alone has made application for 100.

> "Memorandum of Agreement made this day between … of … on the one part, and of the other part. The conditions are that (he) engages to serve the said on a Station, and to make self generally useful for the term of years; obeys all lawful and reasonable commands during that period of the said overseers or authorised agents, be of respectful demeanour, and be answerable for all goods, stock, &c., left in his charge. In consideration of which service, the said doth hereby agree to pay the said wages after the rate of … shillings per month, paid monthly, and to provide with rations at the following rate: — Per week — 3lbs. rice, 5lbs. flour, 10lbs. beef, 1lb. sugar, 3oz. tea. And the said also agrees to provide and pay for the return of the said to the island or place at which this agreement is made, at the expiration of the said term of years. In witness thereof, they have mutually affixed their signatures to this document, the day and date first above written."[41]

---

41 Brisbane Courier 6 August 1867 p 3.

Public Notices.

SUGAR PLANTERS, COTTON GROWERS AND OTHERS.

HENRY ROSS LEWIN, for many years engaged in trade in the South Sea Islands, and practically acquainted with the language and habits of the natives, and for the last four years in the employment of Captain Towns, having brought the natives now on Townsvale Plantation and superintended them during that time, begs to inform his friends and the public, that he intends immediately visiting the South Sea Islands, and will be happy to receive orders for the importation of natives to work on the Cotton and Sugar Plantations now rapidly springing up in this colony. Parties favouring H. R. L. with orders may rely upon having the very best and most serviceable natives to be had among the islands.

HENRY ROSS LEWIN, opposite Donovan's Railway Hotel, Stanley-street, South Brisbane.

H. R. L. particularly requires it to be known that he will be ready to start immediately to the islands, and intends continuing the trade if he finds it answers. Terms—£7 each man.[42]

The Logan, 4 October 1866. Captain Towns received another large addition of South Sea Islanders. They were brought upriver by Mr. Pettigrew's new steamer. The number was seventy. Townsvale plantation was a great success, and 259 bales of cotton were sent away last season.[43]

The success that attended the introduction of South Sea Island labour into Queensland created a demand, and Mr. Ross Lewin made arrangements to supply this class of labour. On 22 August 1867, he arrived in the barque *King Oscar* with 222 natives. The barque was under charter to Mr. Lewin, which started from Sydney. After a fine run of seven days, she reached the Loyalty

---

42 Queenslander 27 April 1867 p 1.
43 Brisbane Courier 5 October 1866 p 2.

Islands and called at Mare, where forty-two men entered into Mr. Lewin's service. The next island visited was Lifou, from which sixty-six men were obtained. The vessel then proceeded to the New Hebrides, calling at Aneityum, and then at Futuna. The schooner also called at several other islands of the New Hebrides. From Sandwich, she received 13 men, from Mai 11, from Tongoa 6, and Tanna 84. All the men spoke English and understood the terms of their agreement to serve for a term of three years with Mr. Ross Lewin, on a cotton or sugar plantation, or sheep, or cattle station. They were to be paid the sum of £18 at the termination of the service with a free passage home. They were also to be fed and clothed during their service.[44]

The *Brisbane Courier* of 7 September 1867 reported on the South Sea Islanders at the Townsvale Cotton Plantation as follows:

> The number of islanders on the plantation at present is 196. Of these, 106 came out in 1864, some in June, and the remainder in November. Sixty-three of the others came out about eleven months ago, and the rest arrived by the *King Oscar*. The time of agreement of those who came in June 1864, expired last June, that being three years since their arrival. They would have been sent back on that date, but, as the time of those who arrived in November 1864 would be soon up. It was thought advisable to keep them a little longer and send home the two lots together. This was explained to them, and they intimated that they were perfectly satisfied. The two lots will be sent back in about a month, and for some time, Mr. Walker has been busy making arrangements for their departure. The carpenters have been at work making boxes for the islanders, to contain their effects, which consist of the prizes they obtained in the cotton-picking season, and the goods they have chosen in lieu of their wages (£6 per year). The assortment will be varied; the men have chosen all sorts of things.[45]

---

44 Queensland Times, Ipswich Herald and General Advertiser 24 August 1867 p 3.
45 Brisbane Courier 7 September 1867 p 6.

The brig, *Heather Bell*, berthed at Towns' Wharf South Brisbane on 2 October 1867. She was from Sydney under charter to R. Towns and Co. to convey 105 South Sea Islanders from the Townsvale plantation to their homes, whose terms of service had expired.[46]

THE SOUTH SEA ISLAND LABOUR QUESTION.

A considerable number of persons assembled in the School of Arts, Queen Street, on 25 November 1867, to hear Mr. R. Short lecture on the South Sea Island Labour Question. A. Macalister, M.L.A., was voted to the chair and pointed out the high importance to every colonist of the issue under question. Mr. Short gave a lengthy speech and quoted the following from a Parliamentary return laid before the Legislative Assembly, by the Colonial Treasurer, on 15 October 1867:

South Sea Islanders brought into Queensland

Location	Ship	Date	Number
Brisbane	Don Juan	18/8/1863	67
Brisbane	Uncle Tom	8/7/1864	54
Brisbane	Uncle Tom	28/11/1864	80
Brisbane	Black Dog	15/12/1865	118
Brisbane	Spec	27/9/1866	63
Brisbane	King Oscar	16/8/1867	225
Mackay	Prima Donna	13/5/1867	70
Bowen	Telegraph	16/6/1865	39
Bowen	Percy	29/9/1866	50
Bowen	Fanny Nicholson	8/7/1867	201
Rockhampton	City of Melbourne	4/9/1867	26

---

46 Brisbane Courier 2 October 1867 p 2.

The total number of South Sea Islanders imported into Brisbane was 607, and at the Northern Ports, 377; making a total of 984. Of these, 201 were returned from Brisbane; but none from the Northern Ports. Since this return, more had arrived.

Mr. Short then quoted from a letter by the senior Naval Officer on the Australian Station dated 25 April 1867 to the Governor of Queensland:

> I have lately received reports of the loss of several vessels, and the murder of several Europeans at Hinchinbrook and other islands of the New Hebrides.
>
> A trader writes: I have been cautioned by several of the chiefs, as the natives seek revenge on the white man for taking the men of the islands and not returning them.
>
> I have sent *H.M.S. Falcon* to visit the islands to communicate with Consul Jones at Fiji, and request him to inform me if natives are conveyed from the New Hebrides to the Fiji Group as labourers; if the trade is carried on by Europeans, and under what licence and superintendence.
>
> I have the honour to request that you will cause me to be supplied with information on the subject of the admission into Queensland of island natives.
>
> I know, from my own experience, that many of the vessels trading to the New Hebrides are manned by rough and very lawless men, who, finding themselves beyond the reach of any civilised power, behave towards the natives with injustice. J. P. Luce, Captain and Senior Officer.

Mr Short went on to add.

> In my letters to the *Courier*,[47] I have stated that the traffic in South Sea Islanders as carried on in Queensland, is a revival

---

47 Brisbane Courier 5 November 1867 p 3.

of the slave trade. Lawless traffic in human beings, colour it, disguise it as you will. It is nothing more nor less than a revival of the slave trade. The Government of Queensland appear to be waking up to a sense of responsibility. A bill has been hurriedly prepared to legalise the introduction of South Sea Island labourers into Queensland and has been entrusted to Dr. Hobbs to introduce into the Legislative Council. They will point to the comparative scarcity, uncertainty, and high price of white labour, and they will argue that it is impossible for them to continue their cultivation, or to carry on their particular industry without a sufficient, constant, and continuous supply of labour of some kind. They will say, moreover, that it will be impossible for them to keep on their estates with white labour because it is too expensive; and therefore, they must have cheaper labour of some kind, get it where and how they may. We are now called upon to consider and decide the principle upon which this colony is to be founded. Is it to be a European colony similar to the other colonies in Australasia, where its industrial operations are carried on by white men—where working men of all classes may find a home and ample occupation for themselves and their families? Or it is to be a colony composed of an oligarchy of white adventurers, with an imported servile black population to carry on the industrial operations of the country? A choice must be made between one of these two principles. You must choose between the white labourer and the black, for the two cannot co-exist together. In no country on the face of the earth can you find a superior race of white men toiling side by side with an inferior race, whether black or coloured. If this principle is adopted, we alter the character of our colonisation. Queensland will cease to be a home for the working man; it will no longer be a field whereby the exercise of honest industry he may attain a position of comfort and independence. We shall undo all that we have done; the immense amount of money spent in introducing immigrants from Europe will have been spent in vain; and the thousands and tens of thousands of Europeans, English, Scotch, Irish, and Germans, who have been induced to come here in the expectation of finding in Queensland an ample field for their industry and enterprise, are to be cast adrift to shift for themselves, or to seek elsewhere the better land of their hopes and aspirations, in order to make room for the cheaper labour of the Polynesian Negro. Queensland, when it ceases to be the home of the industrious white man, will become merely a field for the employment of capital and black labour, to the exclusion of the white. The white labouring population will find no room for employment except by being degraded to the level of the black—a degradation to which they will not submit.[48]

A very large number of persons assembled in the North Brisbane School of Arts on 7 December 1867, to hear Mr. R. Short deliver his second free lecture on the South Sea Island Labour Question. The audience comprised several of the leading citizens, as well as a large number of the working men of Brisbane; and the proceedings throughout were most orderly. The remarks of the lecturer were entirely concurred with by those present. Mr. Pugh, M.L.A., occupied the chair and introduced Mr. Short.

At the end of Mr. Short's address. Mr. Brookes moved that the following petition to His Excellency the Governor be adopted by the meeting and signed by the Chairman on their behalf:

> That your petitioners view with much anxiety the introduction into this colony of a large number of natives of the South Sea Islands, by private individuals, to work as labourers on sugar plantations, cotton plantations, and on sheep and cattle stations.
>
> That these natives have been, and are still being, brought without the sanction of Her Majesty's Government, without any colonial law to control or regulate their introduction, to protect them

---

48 Brisbane Courier 26 November 1867 p 1.

afterwards, or to secure their return home on the expiration of term of service.

That your petitioners have reason to believe that many of those natives have been kidnapped and brought forcibly here, and others under false and deceptive representations; while many have been induced to come by the promise that they should be conveyed home within twelve months; that this promise has not been fulfilled, but, on the contrary, that many of these natives have been detained in the colony for periods of three years and upwards, on the allegation they had engaged for that time.

That this breach of faith, combined with the illegal manner in which these natives have been obtained, has led to the loss of several vessels and the murder of several Europeans at the South Sea Islands by the natives, in revenge for the abduction and detention of their kindred. These facts are confirmed by Captain J. P. Luce, of *H.M.S. Esk*, the senior naval officer on the Australian station, who communicated to your Excellency on 25 April 1867.

Your petitioners regard with dismay the introduction of an inferior and uncivilised race into this colony to supplant the British and European labourers, as it will have the effect of reducing to destitution and inactivity the working classes of the colony, who have been induced to emigrate here in large numbers by the hope of finding in Queensland an independent home and permanent employment; and we would advert to its being irreconcilably opposed to the Constitution of the colony and the intention of its foundation.

Wherefore your petitioners humbly pray that your Excellency will be pleased to use your best endeavours to immediately suppress and prohibit this illegal and injurious traffic in human beings.

The motion was seconded by Mr. Rowland and carried with enthusiastic cheers. The Chairman said that he would lose no time in transmitting the petition to His Excellency, through the proper channel of the Colonial Secretary's office.[49]

The community saw immigration not as a labour question, but as a means of populating the country in such a way as not to pauperise it, but to secure its progress and prosperity. As to mere labour, the community believed a large number of labourers would have to be brought from India or the South Sea Islands — not that they may compete for work with the white labourer, but to do the work unsuited to and unhealthy for the white labourer, or for reduced wages which employers could not afford to pay white labourers. If, by employing Asiatic labour, more capital was invested in the colony and more wealth produced so that the white population was employed in a higher class of industry and better-remunerated — whilst at the same time this dusky race suffered no moral or social deterioration or wrong — then the colony as a whole would be largely benefitted by their employment.[50]

THE CONTROL AND REGULATION OF KANAKA LABOUR.

Unlike the Chinese who were entering the Australian colonies for self-advancement by pursuing gold-digging adventures, kanakas or South Sea Islanders[51] were brought in as indentured labour. Indenture was a form of labour contract; the servant agreed to a fixed term of employment for which he received in return free passage to and from the South Sea Islands and guarantees of work, food, lodging, and medical benefits. However, certain sections of the Queensland community wanted legislation to ensure the kanakas got a fair deal. To highlight the anxiety of

---

49   Brisbane Courier 9 December 1867 p 4.
50   Maryborough Chronicle, Wide Bay and Burnett Advertiser 6 April 1887 p 2.
51   Also so known as Polynesians but were in fact Melanesian.

some members of parliament, on 15 January 1868, Dr. Challinor asked the Colonial Secretary to lay upon the table of this House a return showing:

> (1.) The name, residence, and occupation of all persons employing Polynesian labourers in this colony? (2.) The number of Polynesian labourers respectively employed by the said persons? (3.) The name of the locality (including that of the police district) in which the said Polynesian labourers are respectively employed? (4.) The nature of the agreements between the said parties, and the names of the witnesses to the said agreements?

Mr. Palmer said the Colonial Secretary could not furnish any information respecting the questions asked. He had no means of ascertaining who employed Polynesian labourers or the number of Polynesian labourers each person employed. Nor could he ascertain the name of the locality in which they were employed, or the nature of the agreements they had made, beyond the fact that the wages varied from £6 to £8 per annum.[52]

The Polynesian Labourers' Bill was introduced into parliament in early 1868 and was duly passed and assented to on 4 March 1868. The preamble to the Act read:

> Whereas many persons have deemed it desirable and necessary in order to enable them to carry on their operations in tropical and semi-tropical agriculture to introduce to the colony Polynesian labourers and whereas it is necessary for the prevention of abuses and for securing to the labourers, proper treatment and protection as well as for securing to the employer the due fulfilment by the immigrant of his agreement that an Act should be passed for the control of such immigration.[53]

For those who were desirous of importing labourers from the South Sea Islands after 4 March 1868, they were now required

---

52 Queenslander 18 January 1868 p 7.
53 Polynesian Labourers Act, 31° VICTORIÆ No. 47.

to make application for permission to the Colonial Secretary at Brisbane in the prescribed Form A, stating the number required and how they were to be employed. Such application was to be accompanied by a bond given by the employer in the prescribed Form K, signed by the applicant and two sureties to secure the return of the labourers to their native islands at the expiration of three years or thirty-nine moons from the date of arrival. A licence in the prescribed Form C may then be issued authorising the applicant to import the number required.

For masters of labour vessels bringing in or conveying kanaka labourers to Queensland, firstly, their vessel had to meet prescribed minimum standards: number of passengers, s16; proportion of passengers to deck area, s17; length of voyage, s18; water on the voyage, s19; and provisions on the voyage, s20. On arrival at the port of disembarkation, the master of the vessel had to report his arrival and could not land the labourers until he received a certificate from the Immigration Agent in the prescribed Form L, to wit:

> I hereby certify that the master of the ... arrived from ... on the day of ... 186 ... has produced to me the necessary certificates (Form I) that the whole of the labourers on board have voluntarily engaged themselves &c. &c.

RECRUITS' QUARTERS IN A LABOUR SHIP.

Wawn (1893:4)

On 23 March 1869, John McDonnell, Immigration Agent, wrote to the Queensland Attorney-General:

I have not heard officially or from any credible source of cruelties of any kind being practised on these people. Some of the vessels which are repeatedly named in connection with the Queensland traffic are the following, viz.: the *Syren*, the *Young Australia*, and the *Reliance*. The *Syren* arrived here before the Act was passed and was not, therefore, subject to its provisions. I have, however, visited that vessel as a magistrate and, at the request of the agent; witnessed the agreements, which were explained by me to the men and were clearly understood by them.

The *Young Australia* was not in any way connected with Queensland; she trades from Sydney to the New Hebrides and other islands, taking Polynesians from those islands to the Fijis. The *Reliance* did not sail under the Act, and if she had come here with Polynesians, proceedings would have been taken against the captain, and the vessel would probably have been forfeited according to law.

The Act has certainly not been found to answer all expectations. A measure is now being introduced, which will make provision for the following viz.:

1. The introduction of women at the rate of one-fifth in proportion to the men.

2. The appointment of a Government Agent to accompany each vessel to the islands, and to supervise the proceedings on embarkation, &c.

3. Security for the payment of wages through the Government.

4. Return passages, with Government Agent to supervise delivery of the men at their proper islands.

5. Payment, by employers of men engaged before the Act passed, of amount required for the return, dating from the time of arrival in the Colony.

6. Hearing of cases between Polynesians and their employers under the Polynesian Act.

7. Admission of evidence of Polynesians in such cases without oath being required.

If the present Act were repealed, the Polynesians in the Colony would be in a worse position than they are now, and numbers would be brought here without supervision of any kind. If, however, the new Act passes in its present shape, Polynesians will be under Government supervision from the time they leave their native islands until they return to them again.[54]

The Queensland Attorney-General wrote to Governor Blackall as follows, on 13 April 1869:

> No instance of cruelty, or anything like slavery, has ever been brought under my notice. They seem to be fully aware that they are under the protection of our laws, and in a few instances have brought disputes between them and their masters before the police courts.
>
> The Act in question was passed for the protection of the Polynesian immigrants, and it is feared by many persons that its repeal might leave the labourers exposed to some of the mischiefs described by the petitioners. The Parliament of Queensland has always refused to legislate for the exclusion of Chinese or any race of men; the Polynesian Labourers Act was for the protection of an inferior, ignorant, and comparatively helpless race of men.
>
> It is manifestly out of our power, with our limited colonial jurisdiction, to take any active steps for the suppression of violence in the South Sea Islands. Imperial force will be required should kidnapping, or any other kind of wrong, be shown to be carried on there.
>
> Every effort has been made to secure fair treatment for these immigrants; they have active sympathisers here, and many, who are opponents of their importation, would endeavour to establish a case of kidnapping, violence, or injustice against the recruiting agents or employers if evidence of the kind existed. There are no doubt difficulties in the way of giving them full protection, being heathen, unable to speak our language, and not capable of

---

54 Copy of Extracts of all Correspondence relating to the Importation of South Sea Islanders into Queensland, Colonial Office 5 August 1869, House of Commons paper 408. http://nla.gov.au/nla.obj-2006894992

taking a binding oath. There are, however, a very large number of Christians among them, some of whom speak English, attend church, and through whom there is no difficulty in communicating with a great number of them. This impediment to free communication will be speedily overcome.[55]

On 16 April 1869, Governor Blackall of Queensland wrote to Earl Granville as follows:

4. ... covering complaint made to him by the Rev. Mr. McNair, a missionary stationed at one of the islands of the New Hebrides. I referred these letters to the Colonial Secretary, with a request that a searching inquiry should be made into the case on the arrival of the *Lyttona*, the vessel alluded to; this your Lordship will perceive has been done, and the result throws considerable doubt on the correctness of the Rev. Mr. McNair's statement.

5. In conclusion, there is no reason to apprehend any unfair treatment of these islanders during their employment in this Colony. They have even greater opportunities of making their complaints known than the coolies who are imported into Trinidad or British Guiana from India or China.

6. Nor do I believe that their employment is likely seriously to interfere with European immigration or the employment of white labour; on the contrary, I consider that some kind of coloured labour must be introduced if sugar is to be cultivated to any great extent in the tropical portions of this Colony, which will entail an additional demand for skilled white labour.[56]

Concerning the operation of the Queensland Polynesian Labourers' Act of 1868, the select committee of the Legislative Assembly of Queensland, appointed on 14 May 1869, produced the following report:

---

55 Copy of Extracts of all Correspondence relating to the Importation of South Sea Islanders into Queensland, Colonial Office 5 August 1869, House of Commons paper 408. http://nla.gov.au/nla.obj-2006894992

56 Copy of Extracts of all Correspondence relating to the Importation of South Sea Islanders into Queensland, Colonial Office 5 August 1869, House of Commons paper 408. http://nla.gov.au/nla.obj-2006894992

1. Your committee have taken a large quantity of evidence in order to ascertain what truth there may be in the following allegations made here and elsewhere, through the medium of the public press and otherwise, respecting the employment of Polynesians in Queensland, viz.:

(1.) That they are obtained from their island homes by violence or fraud.

(2.) That they are treated with injustice by their employers, and regarded with aversion by European labourers.

(3.) That, being savages, they are likely to injure our colonists.

(4.) That, being Christians, they are likely to be contaminated by intercourse with our colonists. (5.) That their return to their homes at the end of their periods of service is not likely to be fulfilled according to agreement.

(6.) That their employment is opposed to the interests of European labourers. On these and other points, your committee have made diligent inquiry wherever it seemed possible to obtain trustworthy information, and the result convinces them that these allegations are not proved by the evidence placed before them.

2. Your committee, however, recommend, as a precaution against possible wrong-doing on the part of those who bring those men from the islands, that the Government should send an agent with every vessel licensed for this service charging the cost of such agent against the person to whom the licence is granted.

3. Your committee further recommend that efficient interpreters should be obtained, for the purpose of fully explaining to the men their contracts and duties, as well as,

on their behalf, any complaints they may have against their employers or others.

4. Your committee also advise that Polynesians shall be deemed competent witnesses in courts of justice; due care being taken that they are made aware of their obligation to speak the truth.

5. Your committee find that all employers of Polynesians concur in believing their labour to be highly satisfactory and valuable; and they are of opinion that while the interests of humanity demand that all care be taken of these men, no unnecessary obstacle should be thrown in the way of their introduction.[57]

Furthermore, the Imperial Emigration Commissioners in their report No. 29 of 1869 observed:

In former reports, we have alluded to the correspondence which has taken place on the subject of the introduction into Queensland of natives of the South Islands. The papers have been since printed for Parliament.[58] Before his Grace's despatch could be received, the Legislature had anticipated his suggestion and had passed an Act, which was afterwards somewhat altered and extended, embodying the provisions which he had pointed out as necessary. The principle of those provisions was to place the introduction of South Sea Islanders, and the terms of their contracts, under the control of the Local Government. With this view, it prohibited the introduction of these people, except under a nontransferable licence previously obtained from the Government, and except after inspection of the people on their arrival, and of the contracts made with them, by a government officer.

The Act was met in this country by a comprehensive protest from the British and Foreign Anti-Slavery Society, who denounced it as unconstitutional and illegal and called on Her Majesty's Government to disallow it. As, however, the effect of disallowing it would have been simply to leave the immigration unregulated, the Duke of Buckingham only suspended the signification of

---

57 Queensland Times, Ipswich Herald and General Advertiser 31 August 1869 p 3.
58 See Correspondence on South Sea Islanders HC papers No. 391, 408.

Her Majesty's pleasure until further information was obtained. As the Act had been assented to by the Governor and was in operation, the delay in signifying Her Majesty's pleasure was of no importance. In a report dated May 1868 from the Acting Governor, it is stated that the employment of South Sea Islanders continued to give satisfaction to the settlers in the colony who had engaged them and that the men themselves were industrious, contented, and happy. Up to the date of the Acting Governor's despatch, no complaint of their ill-treatment had been made to the emigration agent, under whose charge they are placed by law.[59]

NEW SOUTH WALES — ROYAL COMMISSION TO INQUIRE INTO CERTAIN ALLEGED CASES OF KIDNAPPING OF NATIVES.

At Sydney, on 27 September 1869, the Commission submitted the following report:

> The allegations contained in the despatch of His Excellency Admiral Guillain (caused) great difficulty, from the vagueness of some of the charges, the acknowledged ignorance with reference to the names of vessels, and the absence from the colony of the captains of the ships whose names are mentioned as having surreptitiously or forcibly removed natives of the Loyalty Islands.
>
> 3. As neither the "Telegraph," the "Edith," the "Fanny Nicholson," the "King Oscar," the "Syren," or "Lyttona" (Latona) have been in this port during the sitting of the Commission, no means have been afforded of inquiring into the accuracy of the specific charges against the captains of these vessels; but the testimony of other masters is uniform that the strongest desire is manifested by the natives, both of the Loyalty and New Hebrides Groups, to leave their homes, either to serve on board English ships, or to labour on the plantations of Queensland; and that any attempt to kidnap them would be not only unnecessary, but most impolitic, and even dangerous.

---

59   HC paper No. 23717.

4. The existence of a migratory disposition on the part of the islanders of the Loyalty and New Hebrides Groups is borne out by the evidence of nearly all the witnesses who are familiar with them.

6. Upon a review of the whole of the evidence, the Commissioners have come to the conclusion that the charge of kidnapping natives of the Loyalty Islands, in the sense of a stealthy or forcible abduction of them from their homes, is not supported by the testimony of the witnesses examined; but Captain Rees, the master of the *Spunkie*, admits that the consent of the French authorities was not sought for, nor, as he alleges, did he know that the deportation of natives from the Loyalty Islands was opposed to the regulations of the French Government.

7. With respect to the charges of Governor Guillain, it appears to the Commission that the evidence taken affords no grounds for supposing that the obtaining of these islanders has been attended either with force, fraud, or deception.

8. The general question of the state and probable results of Polynesian Immigration is one upon which there is great conflict of opinion. Not only those who employ this description of labour, but visitors to the plantations at Queensland and Fiji affirm that the men generally appear to be well fed, healthy, contented, and happy, that comfortable dwellings are provided for them, and that the labour exacted from them is not excessive. Still, it is very probable that in some cases the islanders have left their homes under a false impression of the nature of the engagement they have entered into.

11. On a review of the whole question, the Commissioners think it possible that, under proper regulations, Polynesian labour may be introduced into Queensland with manifest advantage to the sugar and cotton-growing interests of that Colony. All which they humbly submit to your Majesty's gracious consideration.[60]

---

60 https://collection.sl.nsw.gov.au/record/74VKPyrMbagl

On 27 January 1871, Lord Kimberley of the Colonial Office wrote to the Officer Administering the Government of Queensland concerning a letter from the Aborigines Protection Society, dated 3 January 1871, who had formed the view that the Polynesian Labourers Act was so inefficiently administered as to afford no protection to Polynesian immigrants and that the immigration was little better than a slave trade. Kimberley indicated that the allegations of malpractice demanded immediate examination and explanation. A. H. Palmer, Colonial Secretary provided the Officer Administering the Government of Queensland on 12 April 1871 with a report dealing with the allegations of the Aborigines Protection Society. Palmer advised:

> I would also point out to your Excellency that the Society, in their anxiety to prove that the introduction of Polynesian labourers as at present conducted is little better than a slave trade, have gone out of their way to assert what is not the case, and what they have no possibility of knowing, namely, that "the present Ministry are favourable to the trade, and that their advent to power has given it new vitality;" thus utterly ignoring the action taken by the present Government in appointing paid agents to accompany ships employed in carrying Polynesian labourers between the Islands and Queensland, and in framing instructions specially intended for the protection of the emigrants, and for the purpose of checking abuses that might be supposed to exist among the South Sea Islands in connection with the emigration.

Annexed to Palmer's above letter was the following report by Robt. Gray, Immigration Agent dated 6 April 1871:

> Up to this date, 1,634 natives have been sent back to their islands. Of these, a large number have returned and made fresh engagements; and there are still in the colony about 150 whose agreements have expired, and who have declined to return. In some of these cases, they have, through me, placed their earnings in the Savings Bank, to be available at call.
>
> About three weeks ago the *Spunkie* took forty islanders for return

to their homes, sixteen of whom were men who had long since completed their three years' engagement, and who had preferred remaining in the colony to earn more money. These men paid their passage, and although the *Spunkie*, according to the Marine surveyor's certificate, is capable of carrying 135 passengers, the hold was crammed full with the luggage of these men, some of them having as many as three and four large boxes of clothes, besides loose articles of furniture and cooking utensils. The boxes, in addition to clothes and drapery of all descriptions, contained carpenters' tools, such as adzes, tomahawks, chisels, gimblets, hand-saws, butchers' knives; rifles, double-barrelled guns, ammunition, etc. I may further state that within the last two months, over £1,800 in cash has been paid as wages in my presence; and the whole of this money has been expended by the natives in stores, which they have taken with them to their respective islands. I can only now state that there has never been the slightest approach to slavery either in the way in which the natives have been recruited or in the treatment they have received at the hands of their employers.[61]

On 1 February 1871, the following regulation was promulgated under the Polynesian Labourers Act of 1868, Government Agents were to accompany ships employed in carrying labourers between the South Sea Islands and Queensland, and persons making an application were to deposit with the Immigration Agent, the sum of ten shillings for each of the labourers applied for. It was also a condition of the licence that Government Agents were to be provided with a free cabin passage, and suitable provisions and accommodation by the owner or charterer of the vessel.[62]

---

61 Qld V & P 1871 pp 877-886.
62 GG VOL. XII.] 4 February 1871. [No. 13, p 149.

PACIFIC ISLANDERS' PROTECTION ACT (The Kidnapping Act), 1872 (Imperial)

The Queensland government's first attempt to control and regulate Kanaka labour came in 1868 with the Polynesian Labourers Act (Qld), which provided for a specified period of engagement and the licensing of "recruiters." This Act proved ineffective because the Queensland government lacked legal authority outside its borders to enforce the Act. To overcome this lack of legal power and jurisdiction, the British government enacted the Pacific Islanders Protection Act (the Kidnapping Act), 1872 (Imperial), which provided for agents on British recruiting vessels, stricter licensing procedures, and the patrol of British-controlled islands by the Royal Navy; these measures reduced the incidence of blackbirding by British subjects. On 31 August 1872, the Governor of Queensland proclaimed that the Kidnapping Act would take effect in the Colony of Queensland from the date of his Proclamation. The following is the preamble to the Act:

> An Act for the Prevention and Punishment of Criminal Outrages upon Natives of the Islands in the Pacific Ocean. [27 June 1872.] Whereas criminal outrages by British subjects upon natives of islands in the Pacific Ocean, not being in Her Majesty's dominions, nor within the jurisdiction of any civilised power, have of late much prevailed and increased, and it is expedient to make further provision for the prevention and punishment of such outrages. This Act may be cited as *The Kidnapping Act*, 1872.[63]

The Earl of Kimberley in moving the second reading of *The Kidnapping Bill* said:

> At present there was a great desire that those colonies which were suited to the growth of tropical products should be supplied with labour other than that of Whites, and Polynesian labourers were

---

63 GG VOL. XIII.] 31 August 1872. [No. 97, p 1408.

in great demand for that purpose. This immigration of Polynesian labourers was confined principally to the colony of Queensland and the settlements in the Fiji Islands. The immigration to Queensland had been placed under strict regulations by the law of the colony, which provided on the whole an effective manner for the protection of the labourers who had arrived in the colony. But, of course, the Legislature of Queensland could make regulations only with regard to the labourers who had come to the colony and the vessels which arrived within their ports and came under their own jurisdiction. But a system had grown up of late by which vessels belonging—he was afraid to a great extent—to the subjects of Her Majesty went to the South Sea Islands, decoyed the natives onboard, or frequently carried them onboard by force, and conveyed them to the settlement in the Fiji Islands, over which the Queensland Legislature had no control whatever, and where no sufficient regulations for the protection of these poor men existed. He could not help referring here to what he might term the crowning atrocity of the murder of Bishop Patteson.[64] The reason why the natives believed that their confidence had been misplaced was this: These atrocious kidnappers actually made use of signals and disguises to induce the natives to think that the Bishop was about to visit them and to make them come on shipboard: but the result of the stratagem was that when they came onboard they were seized and carried off to the Fiji Islands: So that when the vessel with the Bishop onboard arrived, the natives, under the miserable and melancholy misapprehension that the Bishop was, in reality, an enemy, took their miserable revenge and took the life of their best friend. The guilt, therefore, rested not so much upon the natives as upon those treacherous traffickers who had brought about such a state of mind in these unhappy people. The Bill now before their Lordships would, he hoped, give such power to the cruisers sent to those seas as would to a considerable extent put a stop to kidnapping. At the same time, so vast was the number of these Islands, so large the region over which they extended from east

---

64 John Coleridge Patteson (1 April 1827 – 20 September 1871) was in 1861 selected as the first Bishop of the Anglican Church of Melanesia. He was killed on Nukapu, in the Solomon Islands, on 20 September 1871.

to west, and so great the difficulty of detection, that even with the most active measures and the most efficient laws it would be exceedingly hard to extirpate the practice. The clauses of the Bill had been most carefully framed with a view to the necessary powers, and it was proposed to punish kidnappers in the same manner as under the Slave Trade Acts. With the cooperation of the Australian Colonies, and from the feeling expressed there, we had every reason to expect much good would be done. While the Colonial Government and Legislature would feel that a responsibility rested upon us to do whatever might be necessary, they might be fairly called upon to assist us by their laws and by enforcing the regulations which might be required. There were two or three points in which the Bill might be improved. In the passage of the measure through the other House it was pointed out that it would be very desirable that all those engaged in carrying labourers from those Islands should be licensed to do so under bond so that no vessels not duly authorised should be allowed to take any part in the traffic. Such a provision would give much greater control over the whole system; and though it was not thought desirable to delay the Bill in the other House until a clause to give effect to that suggestion had been framed, he was happy to say he had been able to draw up a clause to carry out that object.[65]

Mr. Knatchbull-Hugessen, Under-Secretary of State for the Colonies, said in the House of Commons:

The Bill did not attempt to remedy every abuse. British subjects had been concerned in these practices; but when the ships commanded or owned by them had been arrested by Her Majesty's vessels, it was impossible to condemn either the individuals or the ships, because it could not be proved that the persons confined in the ships and carried away had been so removed for the purpose of being in the legal sense of the term, employed as slaves. The object of this Bill was to meet that difficulty and to prevent natives being decoyed away by false pretences and under contracts which they could not understand to what was

---

65 House of Lords 3 May 1872 pp185-188, abridged.

practically a state of slavery. Had the provisions of the Bill been law, the *Daphne*, and other vessels of a similar character, would not have escaped, whereas at present the difficulty of conviction deterred British officers from incurring the responsibility of seizures, which might expose them to prosecutions. The Bill provided that it should be a felony to take these natives without their consent and employ them as labourers. There was another point which must not be forgotten. All the provisions of the Bill had been carefully agreed upon with the Australasian Colonies, on whom much of the expense of carrying the Act into force would fall. By an extension of jurisdiction, the responsibility and expenses would be increased, and it would be a serious proceeding to cast that additional responsibility and expense on the colonies without their approval.[66]

The following circular relative to *The Kidnapping Act, 1872* was published for general information:

Dowling-street, 27 June 1872.

I now transmit a copy of the Act which has just received the Royal Assent. Her Majesty's Government were urged, from various quarters, to put an end to the emigration of native labourers, and to forbid altogether the carrying of natives in British ships.

They have not, however, thought it desirable to stop this course, nor does there appear to them to be any sufficient reason why either the natives or the employers of their labour, should be deprived of the benefit accruing to both parties from this emigration, provided that due precautions and safeguards be taken to prevent abuses in the recruitment and employment of native labourers. At present, as you are aware, the only British colony into which these islanders are introduced is Queensland, and the Legislature of that colony has shown a praiseworthy readiness to adopt any measures which are calculated to protect the natives and to secure a thorough understanding on their part of the contracts under which they are engaged for service in

---

66 PACIFIC ISLANDERS' PROTECTION BILL. HC Deb 22 April 1872 vol 210 cc1665-74

the colony. Her Majesty's Government entertain no doubt that similar enactments would be passed by any other colony desiring to avail itself of this native labour.

It has, however, been thought expedient to provide some additional security with respect to the carrying of natives in British vessels; and you will find, upon referring to the Act, that this is effected by sections 3 to 7 inclusive, while by the 8th section, care has been taken to exclude from their operation vessels which have complied with the regulations imposed by Colonial Acts.

The remaining provisions of the Act, so far as they affect the colonies, are substantially the same as those embodied in my Circular Despatch, and it is hoped that the additional facilities for procuring and taking evidence will obviate the difficulties heretofore experienced in conducting criminal proceedings under the Act of 9 Geo. 4. c. 83.

With reference to this point, I would direct your attention to the provisions of the 13th section of The Pacific Islanders Protection Act, by which the Governor of a colony, with the concurrence of his Responsible Ministers, may procure the attendance of a certain class of witnesses and provide for their remuneration.

Her Majesty's Government are fully sensible of the exertions already made by the Governments of New South Wales, Victoria, and Queensland, to check the cruelties practised against the natives, by prosecuting any offenders who came within the jurisdiction of the colonial courts; and they have learnt with much satisfaction from the answers returned to my Circular Despatch of the 20th of April, that the colonial Governments most directly interested in this matter, with the exception of Victoria, from which no final answer has yet been received, are prepared to defray the expenses of prosecutions under this Act if undertaken with their concurrence. This last condition is, as will be seen, practically secured by the terms of the 13th section.

The remaining part of the Act provides for the seizure, trial, and condemnation in Vice-Admiralty Courts of vessels engaged in this traffic, and by the 19th section, the Lords Commissioners of the Treasury are authorised to pay the costs, damages, and expenses which may be incurred in such proceedings.

I have only to add that Her Majesty's Government feel assured that they may rely upon the hearty cooperation of the colonial Governments in their endeavours to put an end to the atrocious practice of kidnapping, which has roused such just indignation both in this country and in the Australasian colonies, and which, if not effectually checked, will bring serious discredit upon the British flag, under which, in too many instances, it has been carried on by unscrupulous offenders. Kimberley.[67]

On 22 April 1872, by letter No. 32, Commodore F H Stirling advised the Admiralty as follows:

Kidnapping South Seas — Queensland.

Where the introduction of islanders is regulated by a colonial Act. It is likely that a few cases of kidnapping do now and then occur without the knowledge of the authorities, and I notice with reference to your letter No. 13 of 3 February 1872 that the master of the *Jason* was prosecuted by the Queensland government in December 1871 and convicted of illegal proceedings of this kind.

3. With reference to your letter No. 17, 14 February 1872, I concur with the suggestion of the Marquis of Normanby that fast sailing schooners might be advantageously employed in suppressing kidnapping, but I am of the opinion that it would require six such vessels each large enough to carry three officers and about twenty-five men and a 20 pounder Armstrong gun. This crew and armament would be necessary to enable the officer commanding to send for trial any vessel he may seize and to meet the resistance which is to be expected from the lawless characters employed in the traffic, as well as to guard against a rising of the islanders onboard in league with the vessel's crew.

Reports have already been received of the large black brig *Water*

---

67 Empire 6 September 1872 p 2. New South Wales Government Gazette 5 September 1872 [Issue No. 246 (EXTRAORDINARY)] p 2294.

Lily commanded by Hayes, well-armed, and of the *Pioneer* described as having two 9 pounders on deck, several guns below and as being a large brig sailing fast and close to the wind. There is also the barque *Anna* or *Hope* mounting a gun and nearly all the vessels employed in the labour trade carry small arms and a large mixed crew of white men and islanders the latter principally natives of Tanna Island.

4. With regards to the number of vessels (six) which I think should be employed I beg to remark that the space which they must necessarily cruise over will be very large. As the illegal acts are checked in one group of islands, they will reappear in others. Thus, it will be requisite for the schooners employed on this service to be about the New Hebrides, Solomon, Caroline, Marshall, Ellice, Gilbert, Phoenix and other groups of islands; also, off Fiji to assist in preventing the landing of cargoes of islanders at out of the way ports and under no proper supervision.

5. The schooners should be supported by ships of the squadron according to circumstances; from whom they could replenish provisions and obtain medical assistance.

7. Having been at sea since the receipt of the last English mail, I have not yet been able to make enquiries about the purchase or hire of schooners, but I may remark that I have not seen any vessels on the Station suitable for the service required. Should their Lordships decide to employ such vessels, I believe they could be speedily built in these colonies and fitted out by the squadron, and that course would be more economical than sending vessels from England. If this plan be adopted it would be as well that the specifications and drawings should be sent from the Admiralty. A special class of vessel would be desirable, capable of carrying a large quantity of provisions and in this respect, schooners would have the advantage over gunboats.[68]

On 24 June 1872, the Admiralty wrote to the Colonial Office enclosing a draft copy of a letter they intended to send to Commodore Stirling regards suppressing the kidnapping

---

68 http://nla.gov.au/nla.obj-1480490269 (Image 308-315, file 6230).

of natives by English vessels and carrying out the Cape York services. The Admiralty advised that the present force of the Australian Station consisted of:

Clio screw corvette 298 men

Cossack screw corvette 275 men

Blanche screw corvette 180 men

Dido screw corvette 180 men

Rosario screw sloop 125 men

Basilisk paddle steamer 177 men

The Admiralty further enquired whether Lord Kimberley had any additional instructions to be given for the guidance of the Naval officer regards kidnapping and that with Lord Kimberley's concurrence, Stirling was to be directed to hire sailing vessels and to employ all ships under his command in the suppression of the kidnapping trade except the two required for New Zealand and service at Cape York.[69]

The Admiralty on 12 July 1872 wrote to Stirling, concerning his letter of 22 April 1872 with a copy to the Colonial Office:

> I am commanded to advise that Her Majesty's government have determined to put a stop to the abominable traffic in question and with this view my Lords desire that you will employ four out of the six vessels now under your orders on this service, instructing their commanding officers to act temperately but firmly in taking all lawful measures for the suppression of illegal proceedings of the nature of Slave Trade.
>
> 3. My Lords authorise you to take immediate steps for building 5 schooners of from 90 to 110 tons, at a cost not exceeding £25 to £30 per ton, ready for sea.

---

69 http://nla.gov.au/nla.obj-1480494717 (Image 319-322, file 6230).

4. These schooners are to have the accommodation suggested by you for 3 officers and about 25 men and for provisions for about 3 or 4 months and about 4 to 6 times of water. For arming these vessels, their Lordships will send out 12-pound Armstrong guns with the required arms and ammunition by an early opportunity and will also send supernumerary officers and men to assist in manning them.[70]

Captain Moresby, *H.M.S. Basilisk* at Noumea on 12 September 1872 reported to Commodore F H Stirling, Australian Station relative to Skull Hunting and Kidnapping:

General Remarks on Kidnapping amongst the Santa Cruz, Torres, Banks and New Hebrides Groups.

Although I have visited every island of any size in these groups, yet the necessary brevity of my stays at each renders my opinions superficial. The larger islands such as Santa Cruz, Espiritu Santo, Mallicollo and others would separately require more days than my visit was hours long to arrive at a satisfactory conclusion.

First. As regards kidnapping amongst these islands, all the evidence goes to prove that it has almost, if not entirely ceased so far as taking natives away by violence is concerned; the cause being that force has been found not to pay so well as persuasion. This is especially the case at all the smaller islands where the natives are a compact body; but on the extensive coasts of Mallicollo, Espiritu Santo and the larger islands, the desperate and unscrupulous characters, such as too often command the labour vessels have still room for their atrocities, as instanced in the case of the *Nukulau* but a few weeks since on the west coast of Mallicollo Island. It is to the lee side of these larger islands that the attention of our cruisers should be especially directed. The masters of labour vessels favourably known amongst the natives often have their regular beats where they can always calculate on procuring a certain amount of labour.

Second. Procuring labour by fraud and false representations.

---

70 http://nla.gov.au/nla.obj-1480504247 (Image 336-342, file 6230).

This is an evil which is gradually curing itself but although exceedingly difficult to prove, I am of the opinion it is still extensively employed to entrap bush natives and those on the larger islands.

Third. The desire of natives to engage themselves as labourers is very fickle, but it may be said as a rule that on every island, more or less numbers are always found willing to emigrate.

Fourth. Queensland is preferred by the natives to Fiji on account of the better pay and treatment, but the cotton plantations of Fiji require much lighter labour than the sugar cane of Queensland.

Fifth. During the hurricane months, the labour trade amongst these islands almost ceases.

Sixth. Special instructions will be necessary for the commander of the next cruiser regarding his actions towards vessels found carrying labour to Sandwich, Erromango and Tanna from other islands for which they can have no licence.

2. As regards the behaviour of the natives, I have pleasure in reporting that in no case have I found them in the smallest degree inclined to be hostile but frequently so afraid that we were not to be trusted that their fears might well be mistaken for malicious intent. I invariably went amongst them, apparently unarmed with one or two trustworthy men immediately in the rear, keeping a sharp lookout. A few trifling presents sufficed to gain their entire confidence except at the islands of Muna, Aurora and one of the Torres groups where they remained shy and distrustful. The two first named islands are those which the *Rosario* punished.

3. I could obtain no fresh information regarding the crimes of Mr. Blair or Ross Lewin.

4. It appears that the frequent murders at Tanna have principally resulted from the injudicious and contemptuous treatment of the natives by the uneducated white men who have settled on that island.

> 5. I am of the opinion that the service amongst these islands would be more efficiently performed by small gunboats than by any other class of vessel.
>
> 6. Excepting the very small islands such as Nina and Futuna round which in even moderate weather, a heavy surf generally sweeps, good and safe landing is to be found during the trade wind season on every island of the Santa Cruz, Banks and new Hebrides groups.
>
> 7. At New Caledonia, I am informed that kidnapping natives has altogether ceased.[71]

Commodore Stirling by letter No. 138 of 7 October 1872 to the Admiralty forwarded Capt. Moresby's report on kidnapping and skull hunting:

> 3. I do not come to the same general conclusions as Capt. Moresby regarding kidnapping in the groups he has visited; nor does information from other sources support altogether his views. The case of the *Nukulau* mentioned in his report is an instance of kidnapping and the *I S Fox* cruising without a licence giving presents to the chief and conveying natives from one island to another is one of those cases of inter-insular traffic which gives scope for the worst form of kidnapping.
>
> 4. The period of the Basilisk cruise was prior to the Kidnapping Act 1872 taking effect.[72]

By letter No. 16 of 24 February 1873, Commodore Stirling advised the Admiralty that the four schooners had been delivered to the Navy and that the schooner *Ethel* would be renamed *Alacrity*. The *Ethel* had been purchased in Sydney as a tender to *H.M.S. Clio* and was commissioned on 1 September 1872.[73] The four schooners, *Beagle*, *Sandfly*, *Renard* and *Conflict*, were

---

71   http://nla.gov.au/nla.obj-1480445480 (image 250-276, file 6230).
72   http://nla.gov.au/nla.obj-1480441903 (image 247-249, file 6230).
73   http://nla.gov.au/nla.obj-1480370612 (image 183-185, file 6230).

commissioned at Sydney on 21 May 1873 with a complement of 28 men per schooner.[74] This made up the five schooners for the kidnapping service.

On 7 July 1874, a meeting of master shipowners was held at the Exchange, Sydney, to consider protesting against the injurious operation of the Imperial Kidnapping Act of 1872 upon the South Sea Island trade. About thirty gentlemen were present. John Campbell was called upon to take the chair, and among those present were Mr. Alexander Stuart, Mr B. Molineaux, Mr. J. B. Watt (Gilchrist, Watt, and Co.), Capt. Broomfield, Mr. A. Campbell, M.L.A., Mr. Merriman, Mr. Charles Smith (McDonald, Smith, and Co.), Mr. G. R. Dibbs, Mr. C. Lett, Mr. Bell, Captains Fairclough, Burns, Maclean, Heselton, Edwards, Sullivan, Punch, and Brodie. The committee said inter alia:

> It was a trade that had been in the hands of the merchants of Sydney, he was going to say for some 40 years. But their worthy chairman had said that as far back as 1806, his honoured firm had been connected with it. This trade of late years had risen to very expansive proportions, and it was of very great importance to the port of Sydney. It employed a large number of vessels, a large amount of capital, and many of their seafaring men; and beyond all that it gave employment to many hundreds and even thousands of natives of the South Sea Islands. The trade had been fairly remunerative to those engaged in it, and it had added very much to the revenue of the port of Sydney, both directly and indirectly. The trade was well worth the while of any Government cultivating, and certainly one that ought not to be recklessly destroyed. But the result of the passing of the Act known as the Kidnapping Act had been for the past two years to transfer this trade from our colonial vessels to vessels bearing foreign flags, and this state of things continued. This was indisputable. Everyone connected with the South Sea Island trade knew that it was a fact, that whereas in former years there was scarcely a vessel engaged in this trade except those from the

---

74 http://nla.gov.au/nla.obj-1481736126 (image 95, file 6261).

port of Sydney, there was now a larger number of vessels carrying foreign flags engaged in it. Was this a state of things that ought to be allowed to exist? Or was it necessary that it should exist? It seemed to him that it had been brought about entirely by the passing of certain clauses in the Kidnapping Act a measure that was passed in utter ignorance of what the South Sea Island trade was and in utter defiance of the very principle of free trade, recognised as such. (Hear, hear.) He said advisedly it was done from utter ignorance. It would be evident to anyone who would read the correspondence which accompanied the Kidnapping Act transmitted to these colonies, or who would take the trouble to wade over the Parliamentary debates on the measure, that the Act was passed in entire ignorance of the legitimate trade carried on here. (Hear, hear.) The trade which he called legitimate, was a trade which had been in existence to the profit of the shipowners and port of Sydney, and to the benefit of natives themselves for 40 or 50 years. But a few years ago, arose another trade, which was called forth by the exigencies of the labour market in Fiji and Queensland. That trade, instead of employing the natives of the South Sea Islands in those seafaring occupations which were natural to them, and to which they had been brought up from their youth, took them from one place to another, and there being no regulation on the part of either of the Imperial or the Colonial authorities, many abuses were developed. Such a case as that of the *Carl* was enough to make men take some action in the matter. But instead of inquiring into the actual state of the relations between this colony and the South Sea Islands; the atrocities-and he could call them by no other name that were committed by that vessel, and in one or two other notorious cases-were seized upon at home and made the text upon which the Kidnapping Act was passed. The effect of the Act, though he did not say the intention, had been to put a stop to the whole trade. The trade in the islanders, right enough in its original conception, though it grew into a great abuse had not only been stopped, but the legitimate trade had been destroyed. The circumstances affecting this trade were known as being contained in the third clause of the Act, which enacted that "it shall not be lawful for any British vessel to carry native labourers of the said islands, not being part of the crew of such vessel, unless the master thereof shall, with one sufficient surety, to be approved by the Governor of the Australasian colonies, have entered into a joint and several bond in the sum of £500 to her Majesty in the form contained in schedule A to this Act, nor unless he shall have received a licence in the form contained in schedule B to this Act from any such Governor. About the time that this Act was being passed he had marked this clause, and with others had applied to the Governor here to know what would be done with vessels then engaged in the South Sea Island trade. They had vessels engaged in the trade. They asked the Governor whether he would grant them a licence. The Governor said, "No, I cannot grant you a licence; wait until the Act is passed." The Act was passed, and they asked the Governor again whether he would grant them a licence. The Governor would not do so and said that the Act did not, in his opinion apply to the crews of their vessels that it was applicable only to native labourers. Even if it did apply to this crew, the Governor said he could not grant a licence, because that could only be granted for the transport of natives from one place to another.[75]

From the above meeting, it was clear that Sydney shipowners felt considerable inconvenience from the operation of the Kidnapping Act. Not only did the Act prevent kidnapping, but it interfered with legitimate trade which for many years had been carried on by Sydney traders. It was customary to employ islanders in the pearl shell and bêche-de-mer fishing in Torres Strait.[76] Considerable correspondence passed between the Sydney merchants and the Government of New South Wales to no avail. They then turned to Commodore Goodenough for assistance.

They asked the Commodore of the Australian Station to issue letters of protection to shipmasters. Captain Goodenough, however, pointed out that he had no power to do this. The terms

---

75 Sydney Morning Herald 8 July 1874 p 3, abridged.
76 See *Bêche-de-mer and the Binghis* by Paul Dillon.

of the Act were precise—"It shall not be lawful for any British ship to carry native labourers of the said islands not being part of the crew of the said ship." This was the hitch. What was wanted was authority to pick up a few here and a few there in the islands; take them off for a cruise to Torres Strait; make use of them for a few months; and then take them back, or perhaps send them back, by the first convenient opportunity, to their respective islands. This was what had been done in former times. Commodore Goodenough replied a protection letter could not be issued except by the special authority of Her Majesty's Government. Until a change was made in the Act, they would be subject to the seizure of their vessels.

THE PACIFIC ISLANDERS' PROTECTION ACT OF 1875 (Imperial).

On 8 March 1875, the Earl of Carnarvon presented a Bill to the House of Lords to amend the Pacific Islanders Protection Act (the Kidnapping Act), 1872.[77] On 16 March 1875, Carnarvon moved the second reading of the Bill and said:

> Its object was to extend an existing Act of Parliament—35 & 36 Vict. c. 19. The principal Amendment was introduced by the 2nd clause of the Bill. The provisions of the principal Act covered only those ships which carried native labour from one point to another for a single passage and did not authorise the carrying in a British vessel of native labourers for the purpose of carrying on the fishery or other occupation in connection with the vessels. It had, however, been found that ships engaged in the pearl fishery and another description of fishery, and therefore following a legitimate trade, employed Natives as seamen labourers, and were therefore entitled to protection. Ships not protected in that way were subject to penalties, and the object of

---

77   HL Deb 8 March 1875 vol 222 c 1388.

Clause 2 was to afford it to those fishing vessels and bring them under the law. It, therefore, provided for the issue of a licence authorising such vessel to carry native labourers for the purpose of carrying on their industry: and it also provided for the due registration of the native labourer so carried. Another evil now existed in regard to these vessels. Inasmuch as they were not under the protection afforded by the Act, and being consequently exposed to seizure and condemnation, they changed their flags and professed to belong to another nationality—by that means escaping the restrictions of the law altogether. This was an evil of a serious kind and had given rise to not unreasonable dissatisfaction. While this Bill would afford protection to vessels sailing under the British flag, engaged in carrying on a lawful trade in these waters, it would not affect, to the extent that was desirable, those ships which were engaged in the slave trade; but he did not know that any Bill could be made completely effectual in that respect until there was an understanding among the European Powers to deal with that traffic in a summary manner. Under the Act, it was provided that the offending ships only should be seized and condemned. In this Bill, power was taken to condemn the cargoes also of such ships. Then with respect to jurisdiction for dealing with these cases. The Bill provided that the High Court of Admiralty and every Vice-Admiralty Court should have jurisdiction to try and condemn or to order the release of any vessel detained under the Act, and gave the same powers as were now vested in Supreme Courts of the Australian Colonies as to the examination of witnesses and the collection of evidence. These were the main objects of the present Bill.

The Earl of Kimberley said he had no objection to the Amendments proposed by the Bill of his noble Friend the

Secretary for the Colonies; for he could well understand that great embarrassments had arisen under his Act to vessels engaged in the pearl and other fisheries. He quite agreed with his noble Friend that the best policy was not to attempt to suppress the labour traffic, but to regulate it. Indeed, it could not be suppressed without the concurrence of the various civilised nations and the presence of a large squadron in the waters of the Pacific Islands.[78]

The Pacific Islanders' Protection Act of 1875 made some important changes to the Kidnapping Act of 1872. It removed the hardship unintentionally inflicted by that Act upon those who were engaged in pearl and bêche-de-mer fishery, thus complying with the petition adopted in Sydney some months previously at a meeting of merchants and others. While removing an unnecessary restriction in one direction, the Act extends the operation of the law to British subjects in all parts of the Pacific, not under the jurisdiction of any civilised power. Thus, it made the law more effective for the prevention of wrong, while abating its needless interference with legitimate enterprise. To give effect to this extended jurisdiction, it was further enacted that power be given to Her Majesty "by Order-in-Council to create and constitute the office of High Commissioner, in, over, and for such islands and places; and to confer upon such High Commissioner, power and authority to make regulations for the government of her subjects in such islands and places, and to impose penalties, forfeitures, or imprisonment for the breach of such regulations."

On 28 January 1876, R. B. Sheridan, whilst assistant immigration agent at Maryborough, wrote to the Colonial Secretary offering his views on the recruitment and employment of Polynesian

---

78 HL Deb 16 March 1875 vol 222 cc 1857- 60. Qld GG VOL. XVII.] 16 November 1875. [No. 135, pp 2298 – 2300.

labour in the colony:

1st. I am not satisfied that in all cases recruits are obtained by their own free will and accord; nor do they in every instance understand the nature and terms of their agreements. I am led to those conclusions by the facts that the men sent as Government recruiting agents are too young, too inexperienced, or too dissipated; hence readily become the tools or dupes of the masters and owners of the trading vessels, whose interest it is to fill up quickly, no matter how the cargo can be obtained; secondly, in very many instances the bargain for a certain or given number of recruits is made with some chief, who, to gratify his lust for the luxuries of civilisation, gives so many boys for so much trade—i.e., beads, tomahawks, old muskets, powder, tobacco, and calico; thirdly, my inquiries convinces me that before their arrival in Queensland, the Polynesians, who have not been here before, do not understand the nature of the so-called agreement nominally signed by them at their native islands.

2nd. The "Polynesian Labourers Act" when passed did not contemplate that natives of the South Sea Islands should be otherwise employed than "as agricultural labourers in the tropical and semi-tropical districts of the colony;" yet, much to the detriment of European immigrants, they fill the places of draymen, storemen, grooms, and of all sorts of domestic servants—even nurses. But the worst feature is being engaged for sheep and cattle stations in the far-off interior of the colony.

3rd. I have grave misgivings as to the treatment Polynesians receive from their employers. Since my appointment, three complaints of ill-treatment have been made to me; in two of the instances alluded to, I am quite certain—although I cannot by white witnesses' evidence prove—that Polynesians were whipped on different sugar plantations. I saw the marks of the blows cut through the skin in one instance; therefore, I suggest that some regulations be made for taking the evidence of South Sea Islanders, otherwise many offences against them must remain unpunished.

4th. There is not any regular system of medical treatment of the

Polynesians on the different Plantations, nor is the cause of death in every case satisfactorily accounted for; whilst as to burial, I am led to believe that the interment of a South Sea Islander in nowise differs from the burial of a dog or any other carrion. I would therefore suggest that a regulation be made, making it compulsory on the employer to produce a medical certificate as to the cause of death; also, that a medical man be appointed to visit every plantation; a small sum per head per annual paid by employers on each islander employed would cover all expenses.

5th. That as almost every Polynesian who dies has some wages due and owing to him at the time of his death, and that as no account is taken or kept of such wages, I would suggest that a regulation be made, compelling all employers to hand over, immediately after the certified death of a Polynesian, all wages which may have been owing to the deceased to the Inspector, to be accounted for to the Government.

6th. With reference to security being given for the return of Polynesians to their native islands sec 6, Form K, Polynesian Act, I would remark, that some time ago it appears to have been the practice to deposit in the hands of the Government the funds necessary for paying the return passage of each Polynesian. Now this latter method has become obsolete, and the bond in accordance with the Act is all that is required; it strikes me that three years' wages, and, say, from four to six pounds return passage money, in all about £24, seems almost too substantial a reason against an Islander's return. I, therefore, think that deposits of passage money, and actual yearly, or half-yearly payment of wages is the best, and safest plan.

7th. It appears to me to be very essential to, and greatly in the interest of the employers as well as the employed, that the Polynesian Inspector should, without notice, from time to time visit the plantations in their districts, and inspect all registers, books, labourers, house accommodation, food, clothing, &c.; also, when deemed advisable, to muster all Islanders, and question them as to their treatment, and hear such complaints as they or their employers might wish to make.

8th. The way in which Polynesians are allowed to supply themselves with firearms, ammunition, bayonets, knives, &c., is objectionable, not only because of the inferior guns imported for their use but because the weapons are used at their native islands for either exterminating each other or to murder white men; besides, there is the constant risk of the gunpowder exploding. Therefore, I think some restrictions should be put in the way of Polynesians obtaining firearms and ammunition.

9th. The South Sea Islanders who come to Maryborough have been taught some of the rudiments of religion by the missionaries; but no effort whatever is made to continue the teaching; on the contrary, a Polynesian who acknowledges that he is a Christian is accused of knowing too much, and hence treated with suspicion and severity.

10th. Much discontent exists, particularly amongst white new arrivals, at the indiscriminate employment of Polynesians in the town; also, because I feel quite certain a great deal has yet to be done towards protecting and befriending the South Sea Islanders, who are capable of much good or great evil, according to the treatment they receive.[79]

The Premier in the Legislative Assembly of 11 July 1876 said the Government proposed to introduce a Bill to amend the Polynesian Labourers Act. The Bill would provide that before an islander was allowed to land from the ship, his employer should pay the price of his passage back to his island to the Government Agent, and that in the event of an islander dying, the amount should be refunded to his employer, provided he proved that the islander had received every attention, and medical comforts. The Bill would also provide that islanders should not be employed away from the coast districts of the colony, and that their wages should be paid into the Savings Bank quarterly. Agitation concerning the proposed bill arose in Maryborough and the government decided to appoint a Select Committee to enquire

---

79   ALLEGED ABUSES CONNECTED WITH POLYNESIAN LABOUR. https://documents.parliament.qld.gov.au/tp/1876/776T195S3-EB87.pdf

into the whole question of introducing Polynesian labour.[80]

REPORT OF THE SELECT COMMITTEE ON POLYNESIAN LABOUR — 1876.

1. The mode of introducing South Sea Islanders into the Colony. With the object of ascertaining the truth of statements which from time to time have appeared in the public press and elsewhere, in regard to islanders beings brought to Queensland, either against their will or in ignorance of the nature of the agreements into which they have entered, your committee examined some of the agents appointed by Government to supervise the recruiting of islanders, they being reliable witnesses who could speak of their knowledge of what takes place before the arrival of the men in the colony. The evidence thus obtained has been singularly corroborative of the willingness of the islanders to come to the colony and of the absence of anything to warrant the assumption that they have been exchanged for trade or otherwise improperly obtained. Moreover, the fact of so many of them have returned to this colony for the second and even the third time proves that they well understand the terms on which they come. In addition to the oral evidence taken on this branch of the subject, your committee authorised the investigation of agents' logbooks— eighty-four in number — and the compilation of a report thereon.

2. Treatment and Inspection of Islanders. Great attention has been given by your committee to the treatment of Islanders employed on plantations and stations in the interior; and whilst they are of opinion that treatment has been, in nearly all cases, humane and kind, they consider it will be satisfactory to employers to have a system of more frequent inspection, which would afford to the Islanders security against bad usage or neglect.

3. Occupations of Islanders. The evidence shows that the

---

80 Maryborough Chronicle, Wide Bay and Burnett Advertiser 26 August 1876 p 2, 31 August 1876 p 2 & 9 September 1876 p 2.

islanders, whether employed on sugar plantations on the coast or stations in the interior, are physically improved at the expiration of their term of service. Nothing has come under the notice of the Committee to warrant the supposition that station life is distasteful to the men; on the contrary, they are represented as being cheerful and contented, and willing to take charge of sheep or to perform the ordinary bush work required on stations. [Vide evidence of Messrs. Rome, Ferrett, Sandeman, &c.] Your committee, therefore, consider themselves justified in recommending that there shall be no restriction as to the part of the country for which the men are engaged.

4. Diet of Islanders. Your committee recommend that where necessary, the dietary scale be amended with a view to the substitution, to a considerable extent, of vegetable for animal food.

5. Payment of Wages, &c. An important matter in connection with the employment of South Sea Islanders is the mode of payment of wages. Instances have come under the notice of your committee where islanders have been unable to obtain their wages, through the insolvency of their employer, until after considerable delay and trouble; and they recommend that the Government, in any future legislation, should make provision for the half-yearly pay of wages, with due arrangement for the return passage of the islander to his native island at the expiration of his contract.

6. Government Agents. Taking into consideration the position occupied by Government Agents, and the responsible duties devolving upon them, your Committee are of opinion that too much, discretion cannot be exercised by the government in the appointment of these officers, and that the rate of remuneration should be such as to place them in a more independent position than they now occupy. The attention of the Committee having been directed to a report by Mr. R. B. Sheridan, the Sub-Inspector of Polynesians at Maryborough, dated 28 January 1876, in which statements of a most serious nature are made, not only, as against employers of islanders but also connected

with the importation of that class of labour, they examined Mr. Sheridan at some length. The evidence of that gentleman proved that his written statements were intended less as a comment upon what had occurred than as a warning of what might take place in future. With one exception, the allegations in his report were not substantiated in any way, and your committee regret that a gentleman of such high standing in the government service of the colony should have allowed his feelings, as a strong opponent of Polynesian labour, to get the better of the discretion which is expected from an officer in his position.

Your committee wish to state that, immediately on the arrival of the *May Queen* at Brisbane, from her last trip, bringing a large number of Polynesians from the South Sea Islands, they took an opportunity of visiting her; and of making a very strict examination of the islanders, as to the method of recruiting, and as to their perfect or imperfect understanding of the agreements into which they were supposed to have entered. Your committee found that, in every case, the islanders perfectly understood the terms on which they came — that no unfair or illegal means had been used for their recruiting, and that they had engaged to come as labourers willingly, and of their own accord; also, that the provisions of The Polynesian Act had been fully complied with in every case. Your committee consider, not only from the evidence of government agents, but from examining the islanders on board the *May Queen*, several of whom had been employed previously at Fiji and Noumea, that abuses exist in the mode of their being recruited for those places, and that the islanders are very often kept beyond the time of their engagements, and receive hardly any wages — one or two old muskets being often the remuneration paid for three or four years' service; and that the many false reports that are circulated about the way the islanders are recruited for Queensland are entirely due to the way agents recruiting for Noumea or Fiji behave at the Islands; and that the islanders thoroughly understand the difference of coming to Queensland and going Fiji and Noumea, and are therefore more willing to come to Queensland. Walter Scott, Chairman.

I wish to add to the above report my opinion that such regulations

> should be made as would prevent South Sea Islanders being employed in towns unmarried, and then only men who have been previously employed in Queensland for at least three years. I would suggest that a larger proportion of wives should be induced to accompany their husbands, both for greater happiness and for the sake of public morality. W.G. Bailey, M.L.A.[81]

The *Brisbane Courier* in an editorial of 24 November 1876 made the following observations on the report:

> The Select Committee appointed to enquire into Polynesian labour have reported. When this committee was first moved, it was believed that the object was to delay legislation rather than to gain information, and the report which is now before us fully justifies that opinion. We are led to believe that, for the production of this report, the country has been put to an expense of about £400, and we cannot refrain from protesting against such an expenditure being entrusted to such hands as the members of this committee.
>
> The question of Polynesian labour in the colony is of vital importance to the community, the sugar planters on one hand, and the workingmen on the other whilst the abuses which are said to exist in some cases in the manner of obtaining and treating these islanders seriously affect the good name of the colony. We consider that the tone of the report, and how the examination of the witnesses was conducted, justify us in saying that no enquiry into Polynesian labour was ever attempted by the committee; their principal object would seem to have been to discredit the report of Mr. Sheridan, the Polynesian Inspector at Maryborough, and to make things as disagreeable for that gentleman as possible. On reading the evidence attached to the report, no one can avoid perceiving the extreme bias of the committee.
>
> Every leading question which could elicit answers suitable for their purpose is asked and reiterated if the first answer did

---

81 Maryborough Chronicle, Wide Bay and Burnett Advertiser 21 November 1876 p 4.

not suit, whilst those questions which might have drawn forth information unfavourable to the traffic were entirely suppressed. The examination of Mr. Sheridan, whose opinions on the subject of this traffic are at variance with those of the committee, was conducted in the style of a cross-examination of a hostile witness by an Old Bailey lawyer and reflects discredit on all concerned in it, except Mr. Sheridan. It was one of the principal objects of the committee to prove that islanders were not bought from the chief and paid for in "trade." For that purpose, every witness engaged in the trade was asked whether the "trade" was given to the chief or the recruits themselves, and in most cases, the witnesses declared that it was given to the recruits.[82]

On 23 December 1876, the government issued the following directions for regulating immigration under *The Polynesian Labourers Act of 1868*:

> (1.) Before any licence to recruit is granted, a separate application, in form A, must be made by each intending employer, specifying in each case one district only within which the labourers to be imported are to be employed.
>
> (2.) All agreements to be entered into on board the ship, on arrival, under the provisions of the 9th section of the Act, must be made with the persons who have so applied for and obtained licences to recruit, and with them only.
>
> (3.) No transfer of a Polynesian labourer by the original employer is to be allowed except after full inquiry, nor until the execution by the intended transferee of a bond, in form K; and then only in cases in which the intending transferor has ceased to require the services of the labourer.
>
> (4.) No transfer of a labourer to an employer residing in a different district from that specified in the original application, under which the licence to recruit was obtained, is to be permitted under any circumstances, until after the lapse of a reasonable time from the arrival of the labourer in the colony.

---

82 Brisbane Courier 24 November 1876 p 2.

(5.) The obligation on the part of employers to pay wages at the end of each year is to be strictly enforced.

(6.) All the other provisions of the Act are to be observed and followed in all respects. R. M. Stewart.[83]

ESTABLISHMENT OF THE WESTERN PACIFIC HIGH COMMISSION.

The British Government established the Western Pacific High Commission by an Order-in-Council in 1877 to extend British authority over British subjects in the islands of the southwest Pacific, then outside any formal colonial control.

> BRITISH ORDER-IN-COUNCIL, for the Regulation of British jurisdiction in the Western Pacific Islands (Friendly Islands, Navigators' Islands, Union Islands, Phoenix Islands, Ellice Islands, Gilbert Islands, Marshall Islands or Archipelago, Caroline Islands, Solomon Islands, Santa Cruz Islands, Rotumah Island, part of Island of New Guinea, Islands or Archipelago of New Britain and New Ireland, Louisiade Archipelago, &c.) and the water within 3 miles of every island or place above-mentioned. Dated at Osborne, August 13, 1877.[84]

In December 1877, Bishop G. A. Selwyn, of Melanesia, wrote to the Queensland government complaining about the quantity of arms and ammunition sold to South Sea Islanders, who took them back to their islands. He added that the evil was a serious one, giving natives an advantage over the white inhabitants, whose numbers they far exceed, and who, if an affray should take place, would fall easy prey to the natives. One individual

---

83 GG VOL. XIX.] 23 December 1876 [No. 84, pp 1418 & 1480.

84 This was an order formally made in the name of the Queen by the Privy Council having the same force in law as legislation. The Order is in fact an extensive piece of legislation.

purchased no less than £6 worth of cartridges. The weapons the islanders took back were formidable, some of them being not merely trade muskets but serviceable Snider carbines.[85]

Consequently, on 6 February 1878, Governor Kennedy, by proclamation, prohibited the exportation to the South Sea Islands of all arms and ammunition, and military or naval stores.[86] On 5 January 1878, in conjunction with the banning of the sale of firearms and ammunition to returning South Sea Islanders, the Queensland government forbade the giving of "trade" to the friends of recruits; no sales or purchases under the form of trade were to be mixed with the making of agreements. It was most necessary that agreements should not be hampered or vitiated by questionable "trade" transactions. This prohibition was reinforced by the following memorandum by the Colonial Secretary, which was issued as an instruction to government agents and others interested in the kanaka trade:

> Statements have frequently been made to me that, in the recruiting of Polynesian labourers, bargains of a very questionable nature are made by the Masters and Recruiting Agents of Labour Vessels. These statements have been confirmed. 'Trade' as it is called, is often given in order to secure the making of agreements. This seems to me to be a form of sale and traffic open to grave objection. In an account of a cruise of the *Bobtail Nag*, which has been written by a government agent and published with my permission, distinct reference is made to 'trade' bargains. From this account, I make the following extract. (Here follows an extract from the "True Story of a Recruiting Voyage" describing the giving of trade to men who are probably owners of the recruits.) I have examined Mr. Nixon, the writer

---

85 B C 24 December 1877 p 2. Wagga Wagga Advertiser 9 January 1878 p 4. Graves, Adrian. "Truck and Gifts: Melanesian Immigrants and the Trade Box System in Colonial Queensland." Past & Present, no. 101, 1983, p 94. JSTOR, http://www.jstor.org/stable/650671. Accessed 23 Apr. 2023. Graves makes no mention of Bishop Selwyn.

86 GG VOL. XXII.] 8 January 1878. [No. 5, p 69.

of the paragraph referred to. He adheres to the opinions he had expressed and states distinctly that he believes that cases of actual sale have taken place. This must be put a stop to. Government Agents, Masters, Mates, and all persons engaged in the Labour Traffic should be cautioned against giving any countenance to transactions of any kind which might be construed into the sale or purchase of any islanders. The passing of 'trade'—muskets, tobacco, calico, or any other commodity of a like coveted by the natives—should be strictly prohibited when a human being, whether belonging to the coast or the island tribes, is in question. The agreements made must not in any way be hampered and vitiated by transactions of a questionable nature. Every facility should be given for the making of agreements, but no sales or purchases of the kind referred to can be permitted. John Douglas. 1 January 1878.[87]

The *Brisbane Courier* made the following observations on the actions of the government over the banning of firearms and trade:

> The question is whether Bishop Selwyn's letter, which we believe led to the prohibition of the export of arms, disclosed such facts as justified the Government in taking that step. We cannot say that we think it did. The Polynesian labour traffic has now lasted for some ten years, and some thousands of these labourers have returned to their islands-all of them taking firearms with them. Under these circumstances, if these arms were employed against either white or black, we should by this time have had some actual proof of the evil instead of the apprehensions merely of the bishop. We think that a trade which has been carried on for years and is not known to have produced any bad results, should not be summarily stopped at the request of a single individual. As regards this proclamation, we consider that whether its promulgation was justifiable or not depends entirely on whether there was sufficient cause shown for the action taken and it will rest with those who approve of it to produce the facts which

---

87 Morning Bulletin 18 January 1878 p 2; Telegraph 15 January 1878 p 2. GG VOL. XXII.] 9 February 1878 [No. 21, p 335.

warrant it. At all events, in this case, the Government had the legal authority to take the action it did; it being, perhaps, open to question whether circumstances required them to exercise it.

In the next instance, however, we doubt both whether the authority of the Government was properly exercised and whether there was any good cause for its use or abuse. Ever since the initiation of the Polynesian labour traffic, it had been customary, when recruiting these islanders, to make presents of what is termed 'trade' to the friends and relations of the men engaged. This had become the regular custom of the trade, and it is believed that the islanders would refuse to engage unless the usual presents were given. To prohibit the passing of trade when recruiting labourers may stop the trade altogether and this, we contend, is a step that the Executive was not warranted in taking without the consent of the Legislature unless great abuses had been proved to exist such as could not be tolerated for a single hour. Now, no such proof was given, nor was it even asserted that any had occurred; it was merely pointed out by a government agent that abuses might occur, and this possibility was considered sufficient to justify action which may cut off the supply of this labour to our plantations suddenly, and without any warning whatever. We are willing to concede that this custom of giving presents to chiefs, or relatives, on the enlistment of a man requires to be carefully watched lest it should degenerate into a system of purchase; but it has been watched by government agents specially appointed, and we cannot see that there is any good reason for believing that any abuses have occurred. We have amongst us several thousands of these labourers, many of whom can speak English tolerably well, and, if anything approaching a slave trade existed, we ought to be able to get absolute proof of it.[88]

On 1 April 1879, the Acting Governor of Fiji, John Gorrie, advised the Queensland government as follows:

> On 29 January last, John Daly, master of the *Heather Belle*, of Sydney, was tried and convicted before the High Commissioner's Court for the Western Pacific, for the attempted kidnapping of a

---

88 Brisbane Courier 23 January 1878 p 3 & 25 January 1878 p 2, abridged.

native residing at Ocean Island. I have since had reason to believe that on the same voyage, an aggravated assault was committed on two natives of what is called Star Island. I have also to state that William Waite, the master of the *Marion Rennie*, of Levuka, was convicted on 24 February of firing at a native of Rue, a small island off Santo.

It may be right to warn the masters of labour recruiting vessels from Queensland ports to be cautious in recruiting on shore at either of these places until they know the disposition of the islanders. I would take this opportunity of suggesting to your Excellency that any extracts from the reports of the government agents of Queensland vessels, calculated to throw light on the condition of the Western Pacific, or of any offences or deeds of violence committed by whites or blacks, could not fail to be useful in the performance of the duties of the High Commissioner.[89]

In keeping with the Queensland government, the High Commissioner for the Western Pacific, on 29 December 1879, prohibited the supply of dynamite to natives of Polynesia.[90]

PACIFIC ISLAND LABOURERS ACT 1880

On 10 August, the Colonial Secretary moved the second reading of the Pacific Island Labourers Bill and said the first clause repealed the Polynesian Labourers Act of 1868. The second clause was a definition of terms, and was pretty much the same as in the present Act, though it made clearer the distinction between a 'native passenger' or 'passenger' and a labourer. The third clause said that no person should hereafter introduce islanders into the colony of Queensland except under the provisions of the Act. The seventh clause provided for a licence to introduce islanders, and although he disliked such a provision intensely, he had

---

89 GG VOL. XXIV.] 19 April 1879 [No. 82 p 961.
90 GG VOL. XXVI.] 21 February 1880 [No. 30 p 413.

submitted to be overruled by his colleagues. Every application was to be accompanied by a bond for return passages, and every importer was also to pay 30s. a head in advance to recoup the expenses of providing government agents. The age of recruits was to be not less than 16 as at present, and they were to have a better vegetable diet. Any islander found by the health officer to be physically unfit for labour should be returned to his island at the expense of the ship. This was a new clause intended to prevent the introduction of labourers in a weak state of health. No transfers would be allowed except under stringent regulations; employers must provide medical attendance, and in the event of the death of an islander his wages due at the date of his death must be handed to the local inspector to be paid into the Pacific Islanders' fund, which was to be established to carry on the Act. However, pursuant to section 4, the above Act did not apply to any Pacific Island labourers now or hereafter employed solely in pearl or bêche-de-mer fisheries on the Queensland coast.[91]

In the course of the second reading speech of the Colonial Secretary, regarding the Pacific Island Labourers Bill, said:

> The fourth part of the Bill related to the care and treatment of labourers when sick. By the 23rd clause, employers were compelled to provide their labourers with medical attendance, when necessary. The least that could be expected of a man who introduced these islanders, regarding the matter from the lowest standpoint, was that he should take care of them. This Bill would give the Governor in Council power to cause a hospital for islanders to be established in any district, and a resident surgeon to be appointed.[92]

As a consequence of Part IV, The Care and Treatment of

---

91 Week 14 August 1880 p 10. Hansard LA 10 August 1880 p 326ff. [Assented to 18 November 1880]; Supplement to the Queensland Government Gazette of 20 November 1880, No. 91, p 1257.

92 Hansard LA 10 August 1880 p 326ff

Labourers when Sick of the Pacific Island Labourers Act of 1880, Islander hospitals were set up in the District of Maryborough;[93] the District of Johnstone;[94] the District of Ingham;[95] and the Mackay District.[96]

In a despatch of 26 March 1881, Lord Kimberley, Secretary of State for the Colonies to Sir A. E. Kennedy, Governor of Queensland, noted:

> The Pacific Island Labourers Act is the only one of these measures that appears to call for observation on my part. The provisions for the protection of the islanders, to their recruiting, their treatment, and their return to their homes, appear valuable and adequate; with the exception that there is no clause limiting the hours of labour. I notice that, under section 33, the wages due at the time of his death to an islander dying while in service are to be paid into the Pacific Islanders' Fund. This does not seem just, if the deceased leaves any relations; and I should be glad with some explanation of this provision.
>
> I would further observe that, while section 14 seems impliedly to prohibit the making of any agreement for service with an islander, except on board ship, upon his arrival, other clauses e.g., 27, 29, 31, 33, 35, 37 appear to contemplate their employment in the colony after the expiration of their original three years' term of service.[97]

THE INTERCOLONIAL CONFERENCE OF 1881.

The Conference first sat on January 13, when all the members were present except Mr. Dick, of New Zealand; he joined the

---

93 GG VOL. XXX.] 24 June 1882 [No. 81, p 1382.
94 GG VOL. XXXVI.] 11 April 1885 [No. 63, p 1196.
95 GG VOL. XXXVII.] 11 July 1885 [No. 11, p 119.
96 GG VOL. XXXIII.] 10 November 1883 [No. 74, p 1250.
97 GG VOL. XXIX.] 9 July 1881 [No. 7 p 126.

Conference on January 20. The Conference finished its session on January 27. On 25 January, the conference dealt with the issue of the Islands in the Pacific. The report of the committee appointed to consider the matter of Mr. Palmer's resolution, and to examine the papers relating to the appointment of the High Commissioner was further considered. The report, as amended, was adopted by the Conference:

> The committee reports that, after careful consideration of the Imperial Acts on the subject of the protection of natives in the Pacific Islands, and the commission to Sir Arthur Gordon, the High Commissioner and Consul-General of the Western Pacific Islands, they have agreed to the following resolutions:
>
> 1. That it is not desirable that the office of High Commissioner of the Western Pacific Islands should be vested in the Governor of any of the Australasian colonies.
>
> 2. That more effectual means should be devised for the punishment of natives of the said islands for any crimes or offences committed by them against British subjects.
>
> 3. That in the case of capital convictions by the High Commissioner's Court, an appeal should be allowed to the Supreme Court of one of the Australasian colonies, to be selected by the High Commissioner.
>
> 4. That more frequent visits of her Majesty's ships among the islands should tend to lessen in a great degree the crimes now so prevalent.
>
> Mr. Dick, Colonial Secretary of New Zealand, dissented from the first resolution.
>
> Mr. Palmer moved, seconded by Mr. Moore. — That her Majesty's Government be moved to take the necessary measures to give effect to the foregoing resolutions.
>
> Western Australia declined to vote, except on No. 2, which the representative of that colony voted for.

At the request of the Conference, the chairman undertook to move his Excellency the Governor to communicate with her Majesty's Government on the subject and to forward the resolution as agreed upon.

APPENDIX TO REPORT OF COMMITTEE APPOINTED TO EXAMINE THE ACTS AND PAPERS RELATING TO THE APPOINTMENT OF HIGH COMMISSIONER.

1. Telegram to the Honourable A. H. Palmer, Colonial Secretary, Queensland.

2. Letter from Mr. Julian Thomas.

3. Papers communicated by *The Vagabond*, Julian Thomas, to the Sydney Daily Telegraph, dated 11 December 1880 and 17 January 1881.

4. Extract from S. M. Herald of 21 August 1880, respecting the massacre of the *Esperanza* crew.

5. Extract from S. M. Herald of 30 September 1880, respecting the massacre of the crew of the trading steamer *Ripple*.

6. Extract from S. M. Herald of 2 December 1880, respecting the massacre of the crew of the *Annie Brooks*.

7. Leader in S. M. Herald of 30 November 1880, respecting the massacre of Lieutenant Bower and five seamen of *H.M.S. Sandfly*.

8. Leaders in S. M. Herald of 29 September 1880, relating to the murder of Captain Ferguson.

9. Extracts from Sydney Daily Telegraph of 3rd, 4th, 6th, 7th, 8th, 9th, 10th, 13th, and 15th December 1880, on the subject of massacres in the South Seas.[98]

---

98 Sydney Daily Telegraph 29 January 1881 p 7. Minutes of proceedings of the Intercolonial Conference held at Sydney, January, 1881. NSW State Library, call numbers DSM/Q354.9/N.

Sir A. H. Gordon, High Commissioner for the Western Pacific, writing from Wellington, New Zealand, on 16 July 1881, provided Lord Kimberley with a review of the work of the High Commission:

> It was intended that the High Commissioner for the Western Pacific should receive extensive and exclusive powers with regard to the control of British subjects, the superintendence of the labour trade, and the intercourse with native tribes within the limits of the Western Pacific. However, the functions of the High Commissioner were confined to dealing with British subjects alone, and the conduct of relations with native states and tribes was confined to a Consul General under the control of the Foreign Office. The superintendence of the labour traffic also, one of the most important functions which it had been proposed to confer on the High Commissioner, was, though given in the first instance, practically taken away by the powers granted immediately afterwards to the Governors of all the Australian Colonies.
>
> It was also determined by Her Majesty's Government that the naval authorities were exclusively responsible for the performance of acts of war against native tribes, and for determining whether such acts were requisite, but that, where it was practicable and would not cause unnecessary delay, the High Commissioner was to be communicated with before action was taken.
>
> The working of the Commission regards the regulation and supervision of the labour traffic, has been almost wholly and absolutely inoperative owing to the causes alluded to above, which have taken all practical checks or means of control out of the hands of the High Commissioner.
>
> As regards the dealing with cases of native outrage, the function of the High Commissioner has been reduced to the expression of an opinion, (if asked for it), whether punishment is, or is not, requisite. I believe that in every case where such a reference has been made to me, I have concurred with the Commodore in considering that it should, or should not, be inflicted. I have very

rarely indeed been consulted as to the nature of the punishment, or informed beforehand what it was to be, but I have in almost all cases considered that the course adopted by the Commodore, or in accordance with his directions, has been just and suitable.[99]

OUTRAGES BY ISLANDERS OF THE WESTERN PACIFIC.

Arising out of the Intercolonial Conference of 1881 wherein recommendations were made regarding the High Commissioner of the Western Pacific Islands, the following copy of a despatch from the High Commissioner for the Western Pacific (Sir Arthur Gordon), was highlighted by the *Sydney Daily Telegraph* given the paper's interest in the administration of law and order in the Western Pacific by Sir Arthur Gordon:

Wellington, New Zealand

22 July 1881

The Secretary of State for the Colonies.

In my despatch, No. 35, of 18 June, I have said, with reference to the punishment of outrages committed by natives in the Western Pacific, I have never, except in the case of the *Dauntless*, had any previous knowledge of the steps about to be taken by the naval authorities for that purpose. This, so far as the actual punishment of offences complained of, is the case; but the sentence may be understood to mean, not only that I was unaware of the particular steps about to be taken, but whether any steps were going to be taken at all. This would be an error, and I hasten to correct any such impression. In a great majority of cases of outrages reported to the Commodore, communication has been had with me by letter or telegram before action was taken, as appears by the accompanying return.

I think that in every case, I have agreed with the Commodore

---

99 HC Command paper C 3641 p 40.

on the question of whether punishment should or should not be inflicted. The nature of the punishment to be inflicted has not often been communicated to me beforehand; but that imposed by the Commodore, or by his orders, has, when brought to my knowledge, appeared to me in all cases judicious and satisfactory. (Signed) Arthur Gordon.

Outrages committed by natives of the Western Pacific Islands from November 1878 to May 1881:

Mystery case of Aoba Island, November 1878, reported by Governor of Queensland and Acting High Commissioner; action taken by *Wolverine*, 19 May 1879; Acting High Commissioner consulted in June 1879.

Murder of Mr. Ingham, at Brooker Island, November 1878, reported by Governor of Queensland; inquired into by *Cormorant*, in March 1879; punished by *Wolverine*, in June 1879; Acting High Commissioner consulted as to punishment, 17 June 1879.

Murder of Robert Provis, at Guadalcanal Island, of *Ariel*, November 1878, reported by Mr. Brodie, master of *Ariel*; inquired into by *Wolverine*, May 1879; punished by *Danae*, in August 1879; punishment referred to High Commissioner.

Murder of James Martin, of *Heather Belle*, at Aoba Island, November 1878, reported by *Wolverine*; punished by *Wolverine*, 20 May 1879; referred to Acting High Commissioner, 25 May 1879.

Murder of Messrs. Irons and Arthur, at Cloudy Bay, New Guinea, December 1878, reported by local papers; punished by *Beagle*, 19 July 1879; referred to High Commissioner, 25 August 1879.

Murder of Charlie, at Marau Sound, May 1879, reported by *Wolverine*; inquired into by *Wolverine*, May 1879; punished by *Danae*, in September 1879; punishment referred to High Commissioner 19 October 1879.

Murder of Jemmy Morrow and one Savo boy at Guadalcanal Island May 1879, reported by *Wolverine*; punished by *Wolverine*,

1 June 1879; punishment referred to Acting High Commissioner 8 June 1879.

Murder of mate and three men of *Agnes Donald*, at Pentecost, June 1879, reported by the captain of *Agnes Donald*; punished by *Conflict* in July 1879; punishment referred to High Commissioner, 30 August 1879.

Murder of crew of *Pride of Logan* at Dedele, New Guinea, October 1879, reported by *Beagle*; inquired into by *Beagle* in November 1879; punished by *Beagle*; punishment referred to High Commissioner, 5 February 1880.

Murder of boat's crew of *Dauntless* at Api, New Hebrides, August 1880, reported by High Commissioner; punished by *Wolverine*, 16 August 1880; punishment referred to High Commissioner, 22 August 1880.

Murder of Jack, mate of *Mavis*, by an Aoba Island boy, one of the crew, at the Island of Tanna, New Hebrides, October 1879, reported by Consul at Noumea; boy escaped.

Esperanza massacre at Ariel Cove, September 1880, reported by local papers; punished by *Emerald*, 8 January 1881, punishment referred to High Commissioner, 15 February 1881.

Murder of Captain Levison, by John Knowles, at New Britain, August 1879, reported by *Renard*; *Renard* inquired into and captured Knowles. Action taken; referred to High Commissioner, 19 October 1879.

Ripple massacre at Nouma-Nouma, August 1880, reported by *Conflict*; inquired into by *Conflict*, August 1880; punished by *Emerald*, 12 January 1881; punishment referred to High Commissioner, 15 February 1881.

Murder of crew of Chinese junk at New Guinea, September 1880, reported by Governor of Queensland; inquired into by *Conflict*, September 1830; No action taken; Chinese to blame.

Borealis massacre, Qualiqualiroo, Malaita Island, October 1880, reported by the *Fiji Times* and forwarded by High Commissioner;

inquired into by *Renard* in November 1880; punished by *Emerald*, 12 January 1881; punishment referred to High Commissioner 15 February 1881.

Murder of three white men of *Loelia*, at Kabeira, New Britain, October 1880, reported by *Beagle*; inquired into by *Eagle*, October 1880.

Sandfly massacre at Nogu Island, November 1880, reported by *Sandfly*; punished by *Emerald*, January 1881; punishment referred to High Commissioner, 10 February 1881.

Zephyr massacre at Choiseul Island, January 1881, reported by trading schooner to *Emerald*; punished by *Emerald*, in January 1881; punishment referred to High Commissioner, 15 February 1881.

Annie Brooks massacre at Brooker Island, November 1880, reported by Adelaide papers; punished by *Emerald*, 17 January 1881; punishment referred to High Commissioner, 15 February 1881.

Leslie massacre, murder of Captain Schwartz at Russell Island, February 1831, reported by *Wolverine*; inquired into at Sydney by *Wolverine*.

Murder of Chinese crew of schooner *Prosperity*, January 1881, reported by Governor of Queensland; information regarding this massacre requested from High Commissioner, 15 February 1881.

Murder of four mission teachers at Kalo, New Guinea, February 1881, reported by local papers and Mr. Goldie; inquired into by *Sandfly* in May 1881.[100]

---

100 Sydney Morning Herald 26 April 1882 p 6 & Sydney Daily Telegraph 1 May 1882 p 3. QSA ITM847061, 82/468 @ folio 92.

LABOUR TRADE IN THE WESTERN PACIFIC.

On 27 February 1882, Lord Kimberley, Colonial Secretary referred Commodore Wilson's report on the Labour Trade in the Western Pacific[101] to the Governor of Queensland for attention and comment. The following are short extracts from Wilson's lengthy report:

> The Queensland Immigration Rules for the guidance of the recruiting agent are very good indeed, but in many important respects, they are a dead letter. For instance, Art. 22 and 23 prohibit any trade or remuneration being given to the chief, friends, or relations of the men engaging by way of barter or purchase; the master or agent doing so being liable to punishment, and the vessel debarred from again going to the Islands. This law is never attended to, as will be seen in the case of the *Mystery* (1878) and the *May Queen* (at Aoba just recently) and others, where the boats' crews were murdered on purpose to get the trade they contained, and I doubt much if a single recruit is obtained amongst the Islands without a certain amount of trade being first paid for him. Again, Art. 41 of the regulations prohibits the exportation of arms and ammunition, yet a Snider rifle and a proportion of Snider ammunition is part of the kit of every returning labourer from Queensland and Fiji. Generally speaking, the Polynesian labourer is well treated on the plantations of Queensland and Fiji.
>
> The rations, too, in Queensland, though ample, are unsuited to the native, who is almost entirely a vegetarian; the sudden change from his natural to large quantities of animal food has the most pernicious effect on him, and is one cause of the enormous death rate, which in Queensland is said to reach to eighty-five per thousand per annum. The native on his island is not accustomed to sustained labour, therefore ten hours a day is too much either to expect or exact. Physically they are not strong, and heavy work regularly continued, added to the change of food and ordinary conditions of life, soon sends all but the most robust to their

---

101 http://nla.gov.au/nla.obj-1359146481 (images 604-624, file 6583), abridged.

graves. But the real and most distressing hardship lies in the way these unfortunate creatures are too often returned to their homes. The Islands of the Western Pacific are but little known; the bulk of them not surveyed their coasts are in some cases not even delineated on the charts, whilst others are not named or even marked on them. Such being the case, some estimate can be formed of the extreme difficulty of finding the exact island and village from whence each labourer was taken. But unless he is not only landed on his island but at his village, he is sure to be consigned to slavery, if not death, as well as the forfeiture of his hard-earned store of trade in return for his three-year labour and expatriation.[102]

On June 20, 1882, the Queensland Premier, Thomas McIlwraith, provided the Governor with a response to Wilson's report for Lord Kimberley's consideration.

> *The Queensland Immigration Rules for the guidance of the recruiting agent*, the Commodore says, are very good indeed, but in many respects, they are a dead letter. For instance, Arts. 22 and 23 prohibit any trade or remuneration being given to the chief, friends or relations of the men engaging, by way of barter or purchase, the master or agent doing being liable to punishment, and the vessel debarred from again going to the Islands. This law is never attended to, as will be seen in the case of the *Mystery* (1878), and the *May Queen* (at Aoba just recently). It is rather remarkable that to find an instance of Regulations 22 and 23 being infringed, the Commodore should have been compelled to go back to the case of the *Mystery*. At the date of this occurrence, the regulations had not fairly come into operation. In the case of the *May Queen*, I have before me the report of the Government Agent respecting the massacre of the Recruiting Agent and eight of the crew of that vessel, but there is nothing whatever in it to lead me to think that Regulations 22 and 23 had been violated, nor has their violation ever been brought under the attention of the Government by any of the Imperial officers. I

---

[102] LA V & P 1882 Vol II, p 575ff. https://documents.parliament.qld.gov.au/tp/1882/882T90S5-67F2.pdf

take leave, therefore, to doubt the accuracy of the Commodore's information.

The Commodore's statement that a Snider rifle and a proportion of Snider ammunition is part of the kit of every returning labourer from Queensland is approximately correct, but I cannot see how a remedy, if desirable, is to be found. At present, there are in Queensland over five thousand (5,000) Polynesians who came to the colony under the impression that at the expiration of their term of three years' service, they would be allowed the privilege accorded to every man of purchasing the articles which he most prizes, of which, doubtless, in the case of an Islander, a gun and ammunition are chief. Any interference by the Government to prevent them purchasing firearms would, to these people, appear, and no doubt would be, a breach of agreement, and I doubt, very much, the advisableness of preventing them investing their money in the purchase of these articles. A gun in the hands of a native is much less dangerous than his bow and poisoned arrow. Knowing nothing of the construction of his gun or the strength of his powder, he hesitates not to use it at any range, and should he succeed in inflicting a wound it is not necessarily fatal. Armed with a bow and arrow, however, it is different. It is the national weapon, and the slightest wound is death. Moreover, the refusal by Queensland to allow these men to take back firearms and ammunition to the Pacific Islands would have no practical effect. At the present time, Sydney alone sends about six times more of these articles to the South Sea Islands than Queensland does.

In the same paragraph of the report, Commodore Wilson says that "the rations in Queensland, although ample, are unsuited to the native, who is almost entirely a vegetarian," Your Excellency will observe from the dietary scale, which will be found in the form of agreement appended to The Pacific Island Labourers Act of 1880, that there are no grounds for this complaint. Whence the Commodore obtained the information, I am at a loss to understand; and although he appeals to the sixth clause of Drs. Wray and Thomson's report to prove the fact that pernicious effects have arisen in Queensland from giving the natives too large quantities of animal food, I cannot find, although I have carefully examined that report, that any such inference can be drawn therefrom; on the contrary, the inference seems to be that they had not sufficient animal food.

He further says desirous of engaging for Fiji are carried off to Queensland, and vice versa; and not infrequently men who only wished to enter as seamen for a few months in what they suppose is a trading voyage, find themselves taken against their will to work on the cane fields of Maryborough. This is a very sweeping accusation to make against the Queensland Government, yet there is not one single case referred to by the Commodore.

I have consulted the Chief Inspector of Pacific Islanders in this colony, who assures me of his personal knowledge that the masters of our vessels who visit the Loyalty, Hebrides, Banks, Torres, and Solomon groups of islands, whence alone recruits for Queensland are obtained, are, with very rare exceptions, perfectly familiar with every beach, bay, and harbour at which either recruits or food may be obtained. Besides this, the Government Agents—some of whom have been in the service for years—know these places equally well. I have not the slightest hesitation in saying, after making the most minute inquires, that the men are in all eases returned to their villages.

In section 7, reference is made to the class of men trading in the Western Pacific. I have previously explained that there are no licensed traders from Queensland in the Western Pacific; consequently, the remarks made by the Commodore on this head cannot apply to this colony. The report of Drs. Wray and Thomson, which Commodore Wilson appends to his report, was dealt with by the government long ago. Since then, fresh legislation has taken place, new regulations have been made, new protectors have been appointed in several districts, and I believe every grievance referred to has been remedied. As these reforms were effected before Commodore Wilson left this colony last year, I think the fact ought not to have escaped his attention.[103]

---

103 LA V & P 1882 Vol II p 607ff. https://documents.parliament.qld.gov.au/tp/1882/882T90S5-67F2.pdf

On or about June 1883, the Administrator of the Government opened the Sixth Session of the Eighth Parliament of Queensland and delivered the following Speech:

> In the event of these Regulations (Indian coolie) being adopted and the labour wants of the Colony being thus adequately supplemented, a happy solution to the embarrassing questions arising out of the employment of Pacific Islanders and a still more objectionable class of labourers, the Chinese, will have been provided. Although my government believes that recruiting by Queensland labour vessels is as a rule legitimately and humanely conducted, and that the islanders are invariably well treated in the Colony, it is unfortunately too true that recruiting is not entirely free from abuses, and that insuperable difficulties are encountered in endeavouring to legally establish the guilt of offending masters of vessels. These occasional abuses have seriously but unjustly compromised the reputation of our Colony abroad, and my Ministers are confident that every well-disposed colonist will participate in the satisfaction they feel at the prospect that ere long the possibility of such abuses will have ceased to exist.[104]

THE RECOMMENDATIONS OF THE WESTERN PACIFIC COMMISSION.

The following extracts are from the Royal Commission into the Workings of the Western Pacific Orders in Council, which reported at London on 16 October 1883:

> 134. We do not, however, think that under proper regulation the labour trade need be discontinued, and are disposed to consider that it is, on the whole, better to organise and regulate than to prohibit it.
>
> 135. Forcible kidnapping is now happily, we believe, very rare, but we are by no means satisfied that it has altogether ceased.

---

104 GG VOL. XXXII.) 26 June 1883 [No. 77, p 1678.

Still, it may, we think, be assumed that no general practice of this sort exists, although occasional instances occur which show that increased vigilance in this respect is requisite.

137. The purchase of recruits is undoubtedly common under various forms; nor is it denied by the labour agents, who say openly that it is essential to the continuance of the traffic. Sometimes presents are made to a local Chief, sometimes to the friends, townspeople, or relatives of those whose services it is sought to secure, but in all cases, they are given with a view of inducing men to enter into an engagement to labour.

138. Misrepresentation and cajolery, we fear, must be regarded as being of well-nigh universal employment, nor can there be any doubt that much discontent and ill-will are frequently created by the breach of promises recklessly made without a thought as to their fulfilment.

139. A total disregard for all native authority is also universal, and is, in our opinion, productive of a very great amount of mischief. To this source, we are inclined to attribute a large proportion of the outrages which have taken place.

147. One of the most unsatisfactory features in the present aspect of the labour trade is the character of persons usually employed as Government agents. The Government agents on board labour vessels are unsuitable and eminently untrustworthy.

150. They know nothing of the languages of the people whom it is their duty to protect, and to inform of the nature of the engagements into which they are entering, and being too often men of over-bearing temper, harsh disposition, drunken habits, and profligate life, not infrequently greatly exceed and abuse their authority. This, we believe, will continue to be the case so long as they are appointed as they now are.

155. We suggest, therefore, that the present mode of appointing labour agents by the different Colonial Governments should cease; that the licensing of vessels should be done away with, and that, in future, licences should be issued by each Deputy Commissioner for his district, the master of every vessel engaged

on a recruiting voyage being bound in the first instance to report himself to the Deputy Commissioner, from whom he should receive a licence setting forth the islands within the district at which he may recruit, and the number of men who may be taken from each. Each Deputy Commissioner should also be authorised to enrol such men as labour agents as would meet the requirements of his district, and whenever he grants a licence to a vessel as suggested by us, one of these agents should at the same time be placed on board.

159. Into the question of the treatment received by the immigrants in the Colonies where they are employed, it is not our province to enter. We believe that it is on the whole, and with but occasional exceptions, neither unkind nor unjust.

IV.—Relations with Natives.

169. The general relations with the natives may be said to consist in seeing that they are not unfairly treated, and on the other hand in striving to induce the natives themselves to prevent theft or aggression and to punish these or more serious offences if they occur.

170. Finally, if necessary, the Deputy Commissioner should declare his inability to obtain redress, and hand over the case to the naval authorities, to be dealt with by an "act of war."

172. Much has been said about the trade in arms carried on through the islands, and Her Majesty's Government has strongly urged its absolute prohibition. We doubt whether it would be possible to effectively check the trade in arms without the cooperation of other European powers, and in these circumstances, we hesitate to recommend its suppression.

173. Much has also been said with regard to the more frequent occurrence of massacres committed by natives, and the difficulty which attends their satisfactory punishment.

174. Murders of white men by natives in the Pacific are in themselves no novelty. That they have frequently, very frequently, been perpetrated, and that there have always been Islands at

which it was impossible to land without incurring the most imminent hazard. They are due, in almost every case, to one of three exciting causes—cupidity, revenge, or fear.

175. Cupidity is strong in the ordinary savage, and he will gratify his desire for acquisition if he sees the means of doing so without immediate risk to himself.

176. The desire for revenge, not on the individual offender but on any member of his tribe or race, is perhaps the commonest cause of outrages committed by natives and has been so since the days of their earliest intercourse with whites.

177. Fear of the unknown influences, and possibly magical powers of white men undoubtedly has in many cases led to their murder, and probably largely felt on those islands where no stranger is allowed to land.

178. But the question now before us is not why murders are committed, but why they have become

of more frequent occurrence than was the case in times past.

179. We consider the increased number of murders committed in the Western Pacific to be due chiefly to four causes:

1. There is now a far greater frequency of intercourse between whites and natives than was formerly the case, and the opportunities for murder, and temptations to commit it, are consequently multiplied in the same ratio.

2. Owing to this greater frequency of intercourse, the natives have lost much of the awe in which whites were formerly held by them.

3. The possession of firearms and ammunition by the natives has given them a confidence and boldness they did not before possess and enables them to inflict death from far greater distances, and with far less risk to themselves than was formerly the case.

4. A large number of murders is also due to the criminal carelessness of the traders and the total disregard on their part

of the precautions formerly observed in all communications with the natives, as well as to the small size of the vessels now often employed in the Pacific trade.

181. We think it highly desirable that in cases of outrages committed by natives against whites, jurisdiction should by Act of the Imperial Parliament be conferred on the High Commissioner's Court.

185. In many instances, it will be found impossible to deal by acts of war with offences that yet may well merit punishment, and in the absence of any legal jurisdiction over offenders in such cases, the course to be pursued with respect to them is perplexing in the extreme, and the adoption of any mode of action whatever surrounded with well-nigh insurmountable difficulties. The grant of such jurisdiction would in no respect diminish the power of the naval officer commanding in the locality to proceed to acts of war or lessen his responsibility for undertaking them.[105]

We recommend that the Orders-in-Council should be carefully revised, with a view to their simplification.

As regards the labour trade,

We recommend—and consider it essential to the continued sufferance of the trade—that its regulation should be placed entirely under imperial authority.

To effect this, we advise (1) the appointment of a greatly superior class of labour agents, to be nominated and paid by the Imperial authorities, conjointly with the owners of the labour vessels as before suggested; (2) that every colonial vessel starting on a labour cruise should be compelled, in the first instance, to report to the Deputy Commissioner of the district within which he proposes to recruit, and to receive from him a recruiting agent and a licence, stating at what islands and for what number of men permission to recruit is given; (3) that when recruiting is completed the vessel should return to the Deputy Commissioner, discharge the labour agent, and report proceedings during the

---

105 https://documents.parliament.qld.gov.au/tp/1884/984T15S2-54BC.pdf

cruise, and that, after having discharged the labour agent, the vessel shall be bound under heavy penalties to proceed direct to her destination; (4) that when labour is returned, a similar process should be gone through.

We recommend, further, that the recruiting of women should be limited strictly to wives or immediate relations of men recruited, and conveyed in the same vessel and at the same time as themselves.

We cannot conclude this report without again expressing our firm conviction that any considerable delay in placing upon a more satisfactory footing the control over British subjects in the Western Pacific, and the supervision of their relations and intercourse with the native races, will be perilous, and, in all probability, attended with calamitous results. (Signed) Arthur Gordon. A. H. Hoskins. J. O. Wilson.[106]

THE PACIFIC ISLAND LABOURERS ACT OF 1880 AMENDMENT ACT OF 1884.

On 23 January 1884 at the second reading speech, the Premier (S. W. Griffith) said:

> Mr. Speaker, this Bill deals with one very important phase of the Labour question. Last week we passed through this House a Bill removing from our statute book the Acts which recognised the possibility or probability of our having recourse to India as a source of supply for agricultural labour. This Bill is framed to include all islanders alike, whether under their three years indentures or if their indentures have expired. One of the great evils complained of, and it is a very serious one, is that the Polynesians, the excuse for whose introduction here is that Europeans cannot be found to do the necessary work that they are doing, are not confined to the work for which they were introduced. The excuse is merely used as a pretext. People

---

106 Queenslander 12 July 1884 p 67.

are induced to tolerate their introduction on this pretext; but when the islanders are once here, they are employed in all sorts of occupations: engine drivers, grooms, coachmen, domestic servants, carters, and nurses. They are engaged in all these and other occupations. They would certainly not be allowed to be introduced to engage in any of those occupations. To tolerate the introduction of these islanders is only a temporary measure. I wish everybody to understand that it can only be a temporary measure, that is, the permission for their introduction at all. But while they are here, I think that they ought to be confined to fieldwork. There are no provisions in the present law relating to time-expired kanakas: they are free to go anywhere, and they are engaged in all sorts of occupations. They are engaged as splitters, fencers, carriers, and grooms; in fact, there is scarcely any occupation in which they are not engaged. We propose, therefore, to restrict their occupation to what we call proper fieldwork which is work which many persons insist the kanakas are the only persons on earth who can be found to do. To define "fieldwork" is a difficult thing; and probably there will be some difference of opinion about the 2nd clause in the Bill, in which it is said that fieldwork shall not include-

"The working of or attending upon machinery used in making the products thereof marketable; the business of grooms or coachmen; the business of horse-driving or carting, except in fieldwork; or domestic or household service."

I think there will be no difference of opinion on this point that the business of grooms or coachmen and horse-driving or carting is not fieldwork. I have seen half-a-mile of drays all driven by kanakas, and it is no use telling me that that is work that cannot be done by white men. The 2nd clause and the clauses corresponding to it clauses 7, 8, and 9 deal with the employment of Polynesians in other than fieldwork. Other parts of the Bill deal with other scandals. There is no doubt that the administration of the Polynesian Labourers Act has been, and is up to the present time, extremely defective. Most serious abuses exist in the labour trade. The 6th clause raises another question that it shall not be lawful to supply Polynesians with firearms. What do we find now in the South Sea Islands? They are becoming full of firearms, and when peaceable traders going there from here or elsewhere come near their shores or come round a point perhaps, they are met with a volley of rifle bullets. Another matter I must now refer to is dealt with by the 12th section. The present Act does not apply to islanders engaged in the pearl or bêche-de-mer fisheries at all. The 42nd section of the principal Act, which included a prohibition against supplying spirits to islanders, did not consequently apply to those employed in the fisheries; but, from the reports I have received sometimes from Torres Strait, most terrible orgies occur from the supply of spirits to Polynesians engaged in the boats fishing there. I think it better to put a stop to them, and for that reason, the clause has been inserted in the Bill.[107]

REGULATIONS OF THE PACIFIC ISLAND LABOURERS ACT OF 1880.

On 17 April 1884, the Colonial Secretary's Office published Regulations and General Instructions to Government Agents pursuant to *The Pacific Island Labourers Act of 1880*.[108]

On 24 June 1884, the Colonial Secretary's Office advised that the High Commissioner for the Western Pacific had prohibited the supply of arms, ammunition, etc., to natives of the Western Pacific Islands. And, further, this Regulation would not be presumed against vessels until September 1st, unless they had left a port in any Australasian Colony more than one month

---

107 Hansard, LA, 23 January 1884 p 133, abridged; [assented to 10 March 1884]; Supplement to the Queensland G Gazette, 10 March, 1884, No. 44, p 787. Regulations, GG VOL. XXXIV.] 18 April 1884, [No. 66, p 1151 & 1231; Brisbane Courier 19 January 1884 p 5; Warwick Argus 22 April 1884 p 2.
108 GG VOL. XXXIV.] 18 April 1884 [No. 66, p 1158.

after the publication of the Regulation in such Colony.[109]

By a notice in the Queensland government gazette of 19 June 1884, the Colonial Secretary of Queensland forbad the recruiting of Pacific Island Labourers at the islands of New Britain and New Ireland, and the small islands adjacent thereto; at the island of New Guinea, and the small islands adjacent thereto; and at any of the islands within the Louisiade Archipelago.[110] And by a further notice in the Queensland gazette of 24 December 1884, it was notified for general information that recruiting of Pacific Island Labourers had been prohibited within the limits of the British Protectorate of New Guinea, the boundaries of which were described in the schedule to the Proclamation issued by Commodore Erskine on 6 November 1884.[111]

ALLEGED KIDNAPPING IN THE LOUISIADES.

The Rev. J Chalmers forwarded a letter to the Colonial Secretary, in which he enclosed a report of kidnapping said to have taken place in the Louisiade Group. The cutter *Eileen* had reported to Rev. W. G. Lawes that she had touched several islands in the group and found them nearly depopulated. The natives stated that a large three-masted vessel came and took away nearly all the men. It was subsequently pointed out that the *Ceara* had obtained 107 recruits in thirty-eight days, and that they were from the southeast corner of New Guinea. Upon application being made for fresh licences, the acting Immigration Agent directed that an inquiry should be made into her last two voyages. The inquiry was held by Mr. E. Morey, police magistrate of Townsville, who reported as follows:

---

109 GG VOL. XXXIV.] 28 June 1884 [No. 102, pp 1956-1957.
110 GG VOL. XXXV.] 5 July 1884. [No. 1 p 3.
111 GG VOL. XXXV.] 24 December 1884. [No. 114 p 2040

Colonial Secretary

Townsville, 1 July 1884

I submit a report on the labour vessel *Ceara* during her cruise for labour in January and part of February 1884, among the islands of the Louisiade Group.

The charge is that prior to 18 March 1884, a large three-masted ship had visited Roussel, Sudest and several smaller islands, and taken away nearly all the males by driving them forcibly, or by enticing them into the boats and carrying them away against their will, the islands being nearly depopulated by the people of this three-masted ship. It appears from the evidence I obtained that no Queensland labour vessel had visited and recruited boys from the Louisiade Archipelago prior to the visit of the *Lizzie* on 4 January and the *Ceara* on 14 January 1884. The *Lizzie* is a schooner having two masts. The *Ceara* is a three-masted barquentine. The charge made can only apply, therefore, to the *Ceara*. I therefore confined my questions to the main charge namely, kidnapping. That outrage of some kind, if not of kidnapping, had been perpetrated on most of the islands visited by the *Lizzie* and *Ceara* there can be no doubt, for both those ships had reports made to them of ill-treatment. In one instance, the natives complained of a Captain Pryer, or Prior, master of a bêche-de-mer vessel. This is the same man who took away a woman named Murdie from Eaba (Sudest) (See evidence given by Jawille, a native of Eaba.)

There is a Captain Fryer, master of the bêche-de-mer brig *Julia M. Avery*, sailing out of Cooktown. I learn further that George Rotumah, who took the news of the outrages to the Rev. Mr. Lawes, is connected with one Nicholas Minister, master of the *Eileen*, bêche-de-mer cutter. Captain Wawn says that lying reports of the doings and intentions of Queensland labour ships have been spread by bêche-de-mer people for selfish purposes and that the alleged outrages by a three-masted ship (*Ceara*) had its origin in that way. In conclusion, I report that there is not the slightest evidence to show the *Ceara* obtained any labourers on that voyage by kidnapping. Nor is there evidence to show she obtained recruits by any unfair means or representations. Edmund Morey, Police Magistrate, Townsville. [112]

TO THE EDITOR OF THE *BRISBANE COURIER* BY J. FRIER.

Since my arrival in Cooktown, I have seen a copy of the *Queenslander*, dated 9 August 1884, containing the report of E. Morey, Esq, P.M., Townsville, into the alleged kidnapping by the *Ceara* at the Louisiade Archipelago; and also, a copy of the *North Queensland Bulletin*, dated 5 July, reporting the said inquiry. Both published statements are calculated to do me great injury. In reply, I state that I was never at Roussel Island myself, and the *Julia M. Avery* and crew were never nearer to it than Piron Island, about twenty-five miles west, and this was not later than the end of March 1883. After leaving Cooktown last year, I arrived off Sudest on 18 October 1883, landed six natives of Joannet and adjacent islands who had gone with me to Cooktown as passengers only a few weeks before; left there again on 26 October 1883, passing through Smith's passage for the New Hebrides, via the Solomon Islands; arrived off Mallicollo Island on 2 January 1884; paid off and landed my crew at the various islands. With reference to the taking of a woman from Sudest, about the middle of August 1883, when off Sudest getting firewood, the natives of Joannet Island, who had been fighting with the Sibi natives, brought a female captive on board, saying that they intended selling her head to some other tribe. I took the woman from them, intending to leave her at her island, but, unfortunately, a day or so afterwards I was taken very ill with the fever, and fearing for my life the mate brought the vessel to Cooktown. The woman and two of her relatives were a portion of the party of six who I before mentioned had returned to their homes on 18 October 1883.

It seems to me the *Ceara* people are trying to shield their own wrong-doing by casting the blame on the bêche-de-mer getters,

---

112 Brisbane Courier 31 July 1884 p 5 & Queenslander 9 August 1884 p 235.

or else some other vessel has been trading or blackbirding along there after me and has made use of my popularity among these natives to procure labour; for had I chosen I could have filled my vessel. J. Frier, Late master of *Julia M. Avery*. Schooner *Lalla Rookh*, Cooktown, 24 September 1884.[113]

THE LABOUR TRADE.

The Royal Commission appointed on 23 December 1884 to inquire into the recruiting of Polynesian labourers in New Guinea and the adjacent islands including the D'Entrecasteaux Islands and the Louisiade Archipelago reported on 10 April 1885:

> 23. In a letter from the Under-Colonial Secretary accompanying the Royal Commission, we were informed that the islanders, whose introduction into Queensland would form the subject of inquiry, had all arrived during the past year by the ships *Ceara, Lizzie, Hopeful, Forest King, Heath,* and *Sybil*.
>
> 24. This was found to be the case, and we propose to give an outline of the methods of recruiting pursued on board each ship, so far as disclosed by the evidence. This outline will embrace the circumstances under which the natives were induced to go on board ship, the manner in which their engagements, when any were entered into, were explained to them, and their interpretation of the period of hired service.
>
> VOYAGE No. 1. -- *Ceara* sailed from Brisbane on 31 December 1883, and returned to Townsville on 17 February 1884 with 107 recruits onboard. Our opinion is that all the recruits brought by the *Ceara* on this voyage were seduced on board on false pretences; that the nature of their engagements was never fully explained to them; that they had little or no comprehension of the kind of work they had to perform, and that the period for which they agreed to come was in no single instance three years.

---

113 Brisbane Courier 13 October 1884 p 6.

VOYAGE No. 2. -- *Lizzie* sailed from Townsville on 22 December 1883, and returned to Townsville on 17 February 1884 with 126 recruits. We are of opinion, therefore, that not one of the labourers brought by the *Lizzie* on this voyage agreed when recruited, to serve and remain in Queensland for three years; that the nature of their engagements was never clearly explained to or understood by them, and that the method of recruiting was cruelly deceptive and altogether illegal.

VOYAGE No. 3. -- *Ceara* sailed from Townsville on 13 March 1884 and returned to Townsville on 28 April 1884 with 137 recruits. Our opinion is that a system of deliberate fraud was practised in engaging all the recruits during this voyage; that their engagements were not explained to them in any sense approximately correct; and that none of them believed they had agreed to remain and serve in Queensland for three years.

VOYAGE No. 4. -- *Lizzie* sailed from Townsville on 14 March 1884, and returned to Townsville on 2 June 1884 with 67 recruits. On a review of the whole evidence as to recruiting on this voyage of the *Lizzie*, we are of opinion that while some of the natives were forcibly kidnapped, all of them were allured on board by false statements; that the nature of the engagements to which they subsequently attached their marks was deliberately misrepresented to them, and that they had no clear understanding they were coming to Queensland to work on a sugar plantation for three years.

VOYAGE No. 5. -- *Hopeful* sailed from Townsville on 3 May 1884, and returned to Dungeness on 17 July 1884 with 123 recruits. We are of opinion that none of the recruits on board the *Hopeful* were lawfully recruited, and that not one understood he had engaged to remain and serve in the colony for three years.

VOYAGE No. 6. -- *Sybil* sailed from Mackay on 22 April 1884, and returned to Mackay on 6 October 1884 with 18 recruits. We are of opinion that the attempts made to explain the nature of the engagements to the recruits, both at their islands and at the port of arrival, were wholly inadequate; that the engagements were not fully understood by the recruits, and that none of them appreciated that the term of service for which they had left their homes was three years.

VOYAGE No. 7. -- *Forest King* left Brisbane on 17 May 1884, and returned to Brisbane on 31 October 1884 with twenty-one recruits. We are of opinion that all the recruits brought by the *Forest King* were decoyed on board under false pretences; that the nature of their engagements was never explained to them; and that none of them understood they were to work on a sugar plantation for any period, much less for three years.

VOYAGE No. 8. -- *Heath* left Mackay on 19 July 1884, and returned to Townsville on 25 November 1884 with 19 recruits. Our opinion is that the recruits brought by the *Heath* were enticed on board under false pretences, that the nature of their engagements was never satisfactorily explained to them, and that none of them comprehended they were coming to Queensland to work on a sugar plantation for three years.[114]

The reader might have formed the view that there was an inconsistency between what Mr Morey had to say and the findings of the above Royal Commission on the matter of the labour vessel *Ceara*. Captain W T Wawn, who was involved in both inquiries, made the following observation:

> Before I joined the *Heath* as master, I was engaged as a witness on an inquiry held by Mr. Morey, Police Magistrate, at Townsville, in consequence of reports emanating from Nicholas Minister, the bêche-de-mer collector.
>
> I subjoin Mr. Morey's Report as it appeared in "The Brisbane Courier." It will be seen from this that Mr. Morey examined several of the recruits who had been brought by the *Lizzie* and by the *Ceara*, as a result of the first voyages of these vessels to the Louisiade; that the recruits had no complaint to make as to the mode of recruiting, or as to the time they were to serve in Queensland. Mr. Morey was certainly much more competent to cross-question these recruits than were the three members of

---

114 Brisbane Courier 4 May 1885 p 2. Abridged. Qld Parl. V & P 1885 Vol. II p 797ff.

the "Royal Commission," who, the following year, declared that all these men had been kidnapped, or had been persuaded by falsehoods to leave their homes.[115]

RETURN OF ILLEGALLY RECRUITED ISLANDERS TO NEW GUINEA.

Taken from the second reading speech by the Premier, Mr. S. W. Griffith of a Bill to make provision for the assessment and payment of compensation to certain employers of Pacific Island Labourers:

> Early in 1884, when I began to discover how the Polynesian Office worked, the first suspicion I had that it was contemplated to resort to New Guinea itself as a source of labour supply was when I was at Townsville. Immediately on my return to Brisbane, I caused a notice to be published in the Gazette, under the regulations prohibiting all recruiting from New Guinea. The prohibition of recruiting from New Britain and New Ireland had been made before, as soon as we knew of the unsuitable character of the islanders and the unsatisfactory nature of the transactions that were carried on.[116] We had not then discovered the details of the misconduct, although in one instance I refused to allow a whole cargo of islanders that had been brought from those islands to be landed, and insisted upon the shipowners taking them back to their islands, which they did. However, the lamentable disclosures made in the *Hopeful* case during the end of last year, and information from other sources that we considered reliable, but which I need not now enumerate, led the Government to the conclusion that there was a great deal more required to be thoroughly investigated, and a commission was appointed to inquire into the circumstances under which islanders had been introduced from New Guinea.
>
> The Commission proceeded to the various places where the

---

115 Wawn 1893, p 334.
116 See GG VOL. XXXV.] 5 July, 1884. [No. 1, p 3. See p 114 above.

islanders from New Guinea and the adjacent islands were employed, and they examined everyone, to the number of about 500. The conclusion of the Commissioners was to the effect that none of these islanders understood the nature of the engagements under which they were supposed to have entered. The Government came to the same conclusion that the men did not understand the nature of the engagements. The question then arose as to what was the right thing to be done with them. They were brought here against their own will and it was the duty of the Government, for the sake of the honour of the colony, to give them the opportunity of returning. Then the Government proceeded first of all to let the men know that they were at liberty to go if they thought fit. Having notified the islanders, we thought it desirable to send them by steamer. We were fortunate in securing the Deputy Commissioner, Mr. Romilly, to accompany the vessel chartered to take the islanders home.[117] When the vessel was chartered, it became necessary to concentrate the men at places where they could be conveniently shipped. Let me here say, lest I forget it afterwards, that a great number of the men brought from those islands were dead and that if the dead men were not accounted for it might have caused a great deal of trouble. We therefore followed the practice which it is customary to observe in trading with these people, namely, that every man must be accounted for in some way. Arrangements were therefore made that the dead man was accounted for by a package of "trade," given to his relatives in his name.

Some of the islanders expressed a willingness to remain in the colony, I believe about seventy or eighty who all came by one ship, and to attempt to take them back when they were willing to remain would have been almost as great a wrong as to bring them here without their consent. But for those men who were willing to go, the Government determined to send. There were then rumours abroad that some of the employers intended to try to prevent the Government from returning the men, and that they would get an injunction from the Supreme Court

---

117 404 boys returned by the steamer *Victoria*, Brisbane Courier 23 June 1885 p 5 & 25 July 1885 Supplement p 1.

for that purpose. Fortunately, no such attempts were made. A gentleman arrived, inquiring on behalf of those employers what the Government intended to do; and I told him at once that the intentions of the Government were to send these men back to their homes at all hazards, and that nothing that could be done preventing the Government doing so. I then told him that every employer who attempted to prevent the Government from performing this duty would be dis-entitled to compensation for any loss he might have sustained by the return of the islanders. Moreover, I said I should regard any such person as having proved himself unfit to employ islanders in this colony, and that as long as I held the office of Colonial Secretary no such person would ever get a licence to introduce Pacific Islanders.

Some persons were misguided enough to make an attempt to retain the islanders by force. I anticipated such an act and had given instructions to the officers to disregard all protests, and to get all assistance from the police and to use such force as might be necessary. In more than one instance, employers locked the islanders up to prevent them from being removed. In those cases, the doors were broken open.[118] Besides this, threats were made to give into custody, as trespassers on the plantations, those who were engaged in removing the islanders; but of course, the police were there to enforce the action of the so-called trespassers, and so all the men were taken away. If those threats had been carried out, the attempts to detain the men, with the full knowledge of the consequences, as I intimated on the previous day, I should have been disposed to maintain that the men were dis-entitled to consideration; but as I have reason to believe that those instructions were carried out in obedience to orders given previously without a full knowledge of what the real position of affairs was, I am not disposed to make any distinction between them and other employers. Now, sir, the men have gone, and we have rid ourselves of that blot so far as we can, and it only remains to decide what is to be done with respect to the employers, who have been deprived of their services.[119]

---

118 Morning Bulletin 2 June 1885 p 5.
119 Hansard, LA 14 July 1885 p 79.

THE PACIFIC ISLANDERS' EMPLOYERS' COMPENSATION ACT OF 1885.

The House resolved itself into a committee of the whole to consider this Bill.

On clause 1, as follows:

> The employer of any islander so returned to his native island may at any time before the first day of January, one thousand eight hundred and eighty-six, send to the Colonial Secretary a claim setting forth the name of any islander so returned, the time when he was introduced into the colony, the cost and expense to the employer of his introduction, the time when the islander ceased to be employed, and particulars of the loss alleged to have been sustained by the employer by reason or being deprived of the services of the islander. Such particulars shall set forth in detail the mode in which the amount of the alleged loss is made up and computed.

Mr. Black said he understood that the compensation provided by the Bill was not merely for those New Guinea Islanders who were returned to their homes, but also for certain boys sent back in the vessel *Jessie Kelly* about twelve or eighteen months ago. Was that the case?

The Premier said that although the Bill was called the New Guinea Islanders Employers Compensation Bill, it was framed intentionally to meet all other cases of islanders returned under similar circumstances. He did not know of any other case except the one referred to, a case brought before the House last year; if there were any, they would be covered by the preamble of the Bill, which specified "certain Pacific Islanders introduced into the colony under the provisions of the Pacific Island Labourers Act of 1880." Any islanders would be included in that category.[120]

---

[120] Hansard LA 15 July 1885 p 108.

Under the Pacific Islanders' Employers Compensation Act, the Colonial Secretary received sixteen separate claims for compensation for the loss of the services of Pacific Island labourers, who were returned to their homes by the Government before the expiration of their terms of service.

Claims for loss of islanders who, having absconded, were returned to their homes:

	No. of Islanders	Amount claimed,
John Bird, Coomera	3	£201
Jesse Bird, Coomera	3	171
William Ross, Coomera	3	318
Hermann Newing, Coomera	1	55
David A Louie, Coomera	4	284

Claim for loss of islanders returned to their homes on the recommendation of the Royal Commission:

Colonial Sugar Refining Co.

Homebush, Mackay	10	£1276
Victoria, Mackay	92	5209

Young Bros. and Co.

Kalamia, Lower Burdekin	23	2022

Drysdale Bros. and Co.

Pioneer, Lower Burdekin	11	1775

Melbourne Mackay Sugar Co.

The Palms, Mackay	16	2030
Alfred Harte-Lloyd, Dumbleton, Mackay	9	3330
James Mackenzie, Seaforth, Lower Burdekin	50	3999
Hamleigh Sugar Co. Herbert River	110	10,646
Burdekin-Delta Sugar Co. Airdmillan, Burdekin	59	1311
Queensland Sugar Co. Johnstone River	1	81
Mourilyan Sugar Co. Mourilyan Harbour	23	1771
Total	430	£37,611[121]

DECREE OF THE GERMAN CHANCELLOR OF JUNE 8, 1885.

The Imperial Commissioner, von Oertzen, published in the Queensland government gazette, the following provisions which would be enforced within the German protectorate of New Guinea:

> 1. New acquisitions of land without consent of the German authorities are invalid, and none but older and justly acquired rights will be protected.

---

121 Brisbane Courier 6 January 1886 p 5.

2. Arms, ammunition, and explosives, as well as spirits, shall not, for the present, be supplied to the natives.

3. Natives are not to be exported from the German protectorate as labourers, except from those parts of the Bismarck Archipelago where this has been done before, and only for employment in German plantations and under the control of German officials.[122]

PACIFIC ISLAND LABOURERS ACT OF 1880 AMENDMENT ACT 1885.

The Premier said the Bill principally related to hospital and capitation fees. The provisions of the Bill were:

- to repeal the provision of the Act of last year requiring a person who engaged an islander whose term of service had expired to repay the £5 passage money to his former employer.
- that the provisions of the Act should continue to apply to islanders from New Guinea, New Britain, and New Ireland, which had now come under the dominion of a civilised power, so long as they remained in the colony.
- to increase the capitation fee payable by an applicant previous to the issue of a licence, to £3; and it was also proposed to increase the hospital capitations from 10s. to 20s., the reason being that the present Pacific Islanders' Fund did not nearly pay the expenses of looking after the islanders, and the matter would, in a very short time, become a serious burden on the revenue.
- that after 31 December 1890, no licence should be

---

122 GG VOL. XXXVII.] 26 September 1885 [No. 49, p 1048.

issued for the introduction of islanders.[123]

The Act was assented to on 10 November 1885 and section 11 provided, "After the thirty-first day of December one thousand eight hundred and ninety, no licence to introduce islanders shall be granted."[124]

THE PACIFIC ISLAND LABOURERS' ACTS, 1880-1886.

On 28 July 1886, the House went into Committee of the Whole to consider this Bill in detail.

> Section 2 Amended the definition of the term "Pacific Islander" or "Islander".
>
> Section 4 Employers were to provide all labourers with medical attendance.
>
> Section 5 Cost of burial was to be paid by the employer.[125]

The Bill was duly passed and enacted on 4 September 1886.[126]

THE STATE OF THE PACIFIC TRADE.

It was reported in the *Brisbane Courier* that for some time complaints had been made by English traders in the South Sea Islands of the wholesale manner in which arms were being sold to the natives by French and German traders. This complaint had been confirmed by every labour schooner returning to

---

123 Hansard, LA, 29 September 1885 p 847.
124 Supplement to the Queensland Government Gazette, 13 November 1885, No. 91, p 1699. [Assented to 10 November 1885.]
125 Hansard, LA 28 July 1886 p 195.
126 Supplement to the Queensland Government Gazette, 10 September 1886, No. 47 p 965.

Queensland. It affected those who desired to trade honestly under the British flag in two ways. In the first place, they were exposed to ever-increasing danger as the number of firearms multiplied and with the natives becoming more proficient in their use; and in the second, foreign labour and trading vessels had an unfair advantage over them, as they easily outbid them both for copra and labour by trading firearms, which the natives in many islands insisted on obtaining. The evil had spread to all the islands in the regular track of trading or labour vessels. The natives had also learnt the difference between the old trade musket and a Snider or Martini-Henry and would accept nothing but breech-loaders, which were readily supplied at an advance of 200 or 300 per cent over cost price.

The recent voyage of the *Flora*, which returned to Johnstone River on 1 January 1886, was an instance of the islanders resorting to the use of firearms. At Tanna Island, where a few islanders had been recruited, the natives made a very serious attack on the boats, resulting in the death of one of the boat's crew. This occurred on 19 September 1885. The occurrence was reported to *H.M.SS. Swinger* and *Opal*, but the commanders of these vessels were unable to take any steps in the matter till they had first inquired into the circumstances, reported it to the Admiral of the Australian squadron, and received his written instructions. The *Opal* and *Swinger* lay for a short time before the island, but, as the weather was too rough to admit of a landing, the "inquiry" was presumably deferred till a more convenient season, and they sailed away. The French war vessel *Allier* was also on the scene; but instead of sailing away, waited until the weather was fine and then inflicted summary punishment on the natives. The next labour vessel that passed saw the effects of this lesson, for the place was as still as death, and not a single native could be seen for miles along the coast. This, it was said, was by no means a solitary instance of the French punishing natives for the slaughter of Englishmen.

At the commencement of 1885, an Englishman named Joe Booth, a copra trader, was murdered at Mallicollo, in the New Hebrides. The English men-of-war would not interfere as he was in the habit of selling his copra to a French firm in Noumea, by whom he was employed. His friends in Noumea petitioned the French authorities to punish the murderers, and a French man-of-war at once sailed for the island, landed a party of men, and after a brief inquiry shot six of the natives dead and took away six more prisoners to Noumea. This lesson had such a strong effect that when an English Government agent landed there shortly afterwards the natives crowded round him in abject terror, loaded him with presents, and begged him not to send another man-of-war. So great was their respect that if he touched a coconut tree, or entered a house, both tree and house were tabooed or made sacred from that hour. The *Flora* also brought news of two other massacres. George Craig, a copra trader, who had lived for five years at peace with the natives on Ambrym Island, bought the schooner *Annette* in Noumea and returned to Ambrym to buy up what copra he could. He bought a quantity about fifteen miles from his old station, and while walking towards his boat was treacherously stabbed in the back with an old bayonet fixed to the end of a pole. He was carried on board the *Annette* and died in the arms of his wife in half-an-hour. The other was that of Peter Coyle, also a copra trader in the New Hebrides, who was shot with a rifle through the head while lying in his bunk on the island of Oba.[127]

ADMIRAL TRYON ON THE PACIFIC OUTRAGES.

Rear-Admiral Tryon reported to the Lords Commissioners of

---

127 Queenslander 6 February 1886 p 233. Brisbane Courier 4 February 1886 p 5.

the Admiralty on 21 January 1887, that the Government of Queensland had shown a practical desire to repress wrong-doers. The report of the Royal Commission of 1885 on labourers introduced into Queensland from New Guinea and the Solomon Islands could not fail to produce good effect due to the scarifying nature of the exposure of cruelty, piracy, and murder committed by white men, and also the cruel conduct towards natives by Sorensen on his last cruise:

> It must not be supposed that all traders in the islands were evildoers. There was ample evidence to establish the contrary. Natives act as a tribe or a community. They hold white men responsible for the deeds of (all) white men, and too often acts of retaliation by natives had fallen on innocent white men; it fell on the next comer who exposed himself. That the natives do not value life as we do, that many were cannibals, that they killed (white) men on certain social occasions such as the launching of a canoe, because of the non-return of natives that have gone to Queensland, or because no payment had been made on account of their non-return had been shown; and it would not be disputed that they had many barbarous practices. The customs of the race, the traditions of their forefathers handed down to them, were still in practice. That they were to be won by firmness and consideration could also be clearly shown, not only by missionaries but by firm yet considerate treatment on the part of others. The experience of the *Lark* and *Dart* surveying vessels illustrated this point and showed that free intercourse and communication with them was not difficult to establish.
>
> How rarely white men guilty of the crimes referred to were punished by white men's laws was well known. The records of the station show there was reason to suppose that the punishment inflicted by natives on white men at times fell on innocent white men, and there was one thing certain when a white man fell, the officers of H.M. ships were appealed to shoot and destroy in revenge; and a section of the Press deplored the "apathy" of H.M. naval officers, who, responsible for their every act, carefully weighed each case before they acted. In some cases, the precise

spot where the offence took place was very difficult to establish. The tribes were very numerous. One tribe was said at times to pay another to punish a white man, so that they may escape from the action of men-of-war, by reporting that the deed was done by a bush tribe that lives probably in some inaccessible or difficult place. Natives cannot be believed when one tribe throws blame on another. Much difficulty existed in obtaining the truth. The man who struck the blow could hardly be held more guilty than those who decreed the sentence; he simply was the first in the race to give effect to it. Again, the wrong men were apt to be given up in place of the real offenders. There was reason to suppose that in some instances men who had been captured from other tribes were sent off as recruits. When men were entered as recruits, the chief received pay in each case, and this had long been the practice. It formerly was illegal (now it was not) to give presents to chiefs, headmen, or relatives, on a recruit being received. Very few cases of disorder had been reported in 1886 in the New Hebrides.

That these acts were due in the main to labour traffic could be shown. To show that the natives were becoming alive to their interests, it was usual for a trader to leave "trade gear" in payment for copra or tortoiseshell, &c, not yet collected by the natives, at different islands and places on his way; the vessels returned and embarked it subsequently. The risk run by traders and by men left at different smokehouses was very great. Admiral Tryon distinctly connected the massacres by natives, with the massacres and evil doings perpetrated by white men previously, and to the labour traffic.

The returned recruits used freely to take rifles and ammunition back with them. The islanders were largely armed with rifles and ammunition and were good shots. This circumstance alone rendered it difficult to act punitively without sacrificing life, and the means that were formerly sufficient to punish were not sufficient at this time. The natives were not wanting in intelligence; they knew how to escape when they had done wrong. Indeed, in many cases, a man-of-war was powerless to act punitively. The importation of labourers from the islands to

> Queensland ceases on 31 December 1890, under the Queensland Pacific Island Labourers Act, 1885, which amended the Act of 1880. When this desideratum was arrived at, the chief and by far the most numerous causes of bloodshed will be removed.[128]

On 4 June 1887, the Colonial Secretary approved Additional Regulations and Instructions to Government Agents, under *The Pacific Island Labourers Act of 1880*.[129]

On 29 March 1892, the Governor opened the Fifth Session of the Tenth Parliament and referred to the following in his speech:

> The condition of the Sugar Industry in the coastlands of Queensland has attracted the attention of my government, and it has become abundantly manifest that a sufficient supply of labour is not available to enable this industry to be extended or even maintained in its present position. Many efforts have been made to encourage Europeans to undertake this work, but hitherto, from various causes, without success. This matter appears to be pressing and to demand immediate action. It is well known that a considerable supply of suitable labour can be obtained from the Pacific Islands, whence many islanders are willing and anxious to come to Queensland. You will therefore be invited to remove the restrictions which now exist upon the importation of labourers, and also to make such provisions to prevent them from competing with European labour in other industries.[130]

PACIFIC ISLAND LABOURERS (EXTENSION) BILL 1892.

On 31 March 1892, a bill to further amend the *Pacific Island Labourers Acts, 1880-1885*, was presented. At the second reading, the Premier said the principal provision was whether

---

128 Brisbane Courier 30 July 1887 p 3.
129 GG VOL. XLI.] 4 June 1887 [No. 24, p 369.
130 GG VOL. LV.] 29 March 1892 [No. 87, 1161.

labourers should be allowed to be again introduced from the Pacific Islands. That question was raised distinctly by the 3rd clause of this Bill, which provided that the 11th section of the *Pacific Island Labourers Act of 1880 Amendment Act of 1885* be repealed. The 11th section of that Act provided that

> "After the thirty-first day of December, one thousand eight hundred and ninety, no licence to introduce islanders shall be granted."

The Bill was assented to on 14 April 1892 and became known as *The Pacific Island Labourers (Extension) Act of 1892*. Section 3 of the 1892 Act repealed the fifth section of *The Pacific Island Labourers Act of 1880 Amendment Act of 1884* and the eleventh section of the *Pacific Island Labourers Act of 1880 Amendment Act of 1885*.[131]

REGULATIONS UNDER THE PACIFIC ISLAND LABOURERS' ACTS, 1880-1892.

Chief Secretary's Office on 20 May 1892 published new Regulations pursuant to *The Pacific Island Labourers Acts, 1880-1892*, and rescinded all former Regulations made in pursuance of *The Pacific Island Labourers Act of 1886*. And further, approved additional Instructions for the guidance of Government Agents to accompany vessels licensed to carry Pacific Islanders.[132]

Chief Secretary's Office issued the following NOTICE dated 11 July 1892:

- forbid the Recruiting of Pacific Island Labourers at the Group known as the Santa Cruz Islands, and at

---

131 Hansard, LA, 5 April 1892 p 100. Supplement to the Queensland Government Gazette, 19 April 1892, No. 111, p 1371.

132 GG VOL. LVI.] 21 May 1892 [No. 19, pp 177-182

the island of Tongoa, in the New Hebrides.

- forbid the Recruiting of Pacific Island Labourers at any place or island within the German sphere of influence in the Western Pacific, that is to say, any place or island lying to the west, northwest, or north of the conventional line of demarcation agreed upon by the Declaration made by the Governments of Great Britain and the German Empire, and signed at Berlin on 6 April 1886.[133]
- rescind the notification published in the Gazette of 16 July 1892, forbidding the Recruiting of Pacific Island Labourers at the group known as the Santa Cruz Islands, and at the Island of Tongoa, in the New Hebrides; and all Government agents and masters of labour vessels are required to take notice of this direction.[134]

Chief Secretary's Office on 13 October 1893, promulgated the following Regulations, No. 55 & 56, in pursuance of *The Pacific Island Labourers Acts, 1880-1892*.

> 55. The voyage of any ship authorised to be employed in introducing Pacific Islanders shall not exceed the period of six months and shall be deemed to commence from the date of the Ship master's Licence authorising such ship to be so employed.
>
> 56. The voyage of any ship authorised to be employed in introducing Pacific Islanders shall not exceed the period of six months and shall be deemed to commence from the date of the Shipmaster's Licence authorising such ship to be so employed. Provided always that the Minister may, on good and sufficient cause being shown therefor, extend the period of such voyage for any further time not exceeding three months.[135]

---

133 GG VOL. LVI.] 16 July 1892 [No. 71, p 727.
134 GG VOL. LX.] 13 October 1893 [No. 42, p 461.
135 GG VOL. LX.] 13 October 1893 [No. 42, p 461.

Recruiting Prohibited — Gilbert and Ellice Islands.

The Governor of Queensland received the following despatch, dated Suva, August 16, 1895 from the High Commissioner for the Western Pacific:

> I acknowledge the receipt of your Excellency's despatch of July 23, covering a report by the Inspector of Pacific Islanders at Bundaberg upon the condition of the natives of the Gilbert and Ellice Islands in his district. The High Commissioner is expected back in Fiji about November next, when the question of the employment in Queensland of natives of the Gilbert Group will be brought before him for consideration; and I would suggest that a further report be made, say up to the middle of October, on the health of the natives already recruited. I enclose copies of orders made by the Resident Commissioner forbidding recruiting in certain islands. These orders apply to recruiting for any place and any employment whatsoever. The question of recruiting in the other islands for employment on sugar plantations remains as it was. The orders referred to prohibit, until further notice, recruiting at the islands of Nukulailai, Funafuti, and Nukufetau, in the Ellice group; and at the islands of Abemama, Kuria, Aranuka, and Maraki in the Gilbert group.[136]

Chief Secretary's Office, on 25 February 1896, published additional regulations in pursuance of *The Pacific Island Labourers Acts, 1880-1892*.[137]

Chief Secretary's Office on 10 March 1896, advised that pursuant to *The Pacific Island Labourers Acts, 1880-1892*, the recruiting of labourers at the Torres Islands for employment in Queensland was forbidden until further notice, and Government Agents accompanying vessels licensed to carry Pacific Islanders were required to see that this direction was obeyed.[138]

---

136 Telegraph 19 September 1895 p 4. GG VOL. LXIV.] 18 September 1895 [No. 69, p 659.

137 GG VOL. LXV.] 25 February 1896 [No. 47, p 472.

138 GG VOL. LXV.] 21 March 1896 [No. 70, p 767.

THE KANAKA LABOUR TRAFFIC. LECTURE BY THE REV. W. GRAY — A MISSIONARY'S VIEWS.

The Rev. W. Gray, formerly a Presbyterian missionary on Tanna delivered a lecture in the Park Presbyterian Church, South Brisbane, on "The Kanaka Labour Traffic."

Mr. Gray, who was warmly received, said that for over twelve years he had been a missionary on Tanna, an island of the New Hebrides Group. He was sent out and maintained by the little Presbyterian Church of South Australia. From the New Hebrides he had been contending with heathenism and worse than heathenism, the evils inflicted on the natives by civilised people who sought their fortunes or profit there. For the first ten years, he was a silent observer of all forms of the labour traffic, and probably his voice would never have been heard on the matter had Queensland not renewed that traffic in 1892. Charges of ignorance had been freely made by both sides. The explanation of that mainly lay in the fact that the Queensland labour traffic had two ends. It had an island end and a colonial end. Much of the bitterness in the controversy had arisen by one party maintaining that because it was bad at the island, it must be bad at the Queensland end. While the other party maintained that because it was good at the Queensland end, it must be good at the island end. That was a mistake which he recognised from the first, and his position had been that the goodness claimed for the traffic at the Queensland end could never compensate for the evil inseparable from the traffic at the island end. Some of those who had said most on the subject on the opposite side had known the least.

The Rev. A. C. Smith, the chairman, spent a month in the Mackay district, and then wrote a pamphlet in defence of the labour traffic which had been scattered far and wide by the Government of Queensland. It was a larger claim than he (Mr. Gray) would care to make that he knew all about the matter because he had seen the traffic in one or two places on a prearranged visit. Still more absurd must be the claim of Sir Henry Norman, when he said, as he did in his despatch of 23 May 1892, that "He had reason to believe that employment in Queensland was very popular amongst Pacific Islanders, and opposition to it in the Pacific was mainly by missionaries and chiefs, who objected to the loss of their people unless they returned with the fruit of their labours." Sir Henry's facts were no doubt seen through the spectacles of his Ministers, of whose lopsided views that famous despatch was an exact echo. Were the objections of missionaries, who had the best opportunities of knowing what the traffic was, utterly valueless?

CHEAP NOT COLOURED LABOUR WANTED.

The supposed need for coloured labour was based on the fact that we had a tropical territory. His experience of Kanakas had convinced him that they had not the power to sustain continuous hard work. If the wages were equal to the work, white men would work in the Queensland cane fields. It was not coloured labour that was wanted, but cheap labour that was not aware that it had any rights. Coloured labour they could get from India. But the labourer knew that he had rights. Cheap labour could be got from Germany, but the cheap labourer would soon become a citizen, with the rights of every Queenslander. The South Sea Islander was not aware that he had rights. The fact was that cheap labour that gave no bother was the reason why there was Kanaka labour traffic in Queensland.

THE SUGAR INDUSTRY.

The Kanaka labour traffic was introduced professedly to save the sugar industry. Was there any certainty that it would succeed? In considering that, two questions need to be faced: 1. What was the future of the Queensland sugar industry? 2. And if it depended on the supply of South Sea Island labour, could that supply be maintained alongside British sentiment? Now the Queensland sugar industry has had fits of depression, which has been attributed to any number of causes, from the want of Kanaka labour to spots on the sun. It was a fact that the price of products had fallen all over the world. Between the year 1880 and the first half of 1887, the wholesale price of fair refining sugar fell 114 per cent. The appreciation of gold, which increased the buying power of gold coinage, improvement in the process of sugar-making, and sugar bounties throughout the world, had all contributed their quota to the fall in the price of sugar. Would it not be well if those interested in the sugar industry were to take stock by looking this question fairly in the face? There was more than a possibility that the sugar industry had in itself the elements of collapse. As the matter stood now, according to the manifesto of Sir Samuel Griffith, accepted by the Parliament and people of Queensland, the sugar industry here depended on the Kanaka labour traffic. The heavy death rate in Queensland, and the limited supply of natives in the islands, made it evident that the Kanaka labour traffic could not go on forever. If the sugar industry depended on the Kanaka labour traffic, the longer it was bolstered up the more ruinous to Queensland must be its final collapse. In any case, it was surely contrary to British sentiment to sacrifice a whole race of people to carry on what everyone said was a losing business.

ABUSES OF THE TRAFFIC.

The missionaries asserted that the labour traffic could not be maintained alongside the British sentiment. He was personally acquainted with the captains, the government agents, and the recruiters. He had seen the work before the days of the *Hopeful* case and since. True, it had been shorn of some of its flagrant abuses, and a better class of men all round was now in the trade. The humanity shown to natives by government agents after the boys were recruited when analysed, was just the care a stock owner would take of his cattle. Every labour vessel, every time it sailed, left behind it a whirlpool of human passion as a consequence of the recruits taken.

THE PRESENT ACT.

The present Pacific Island Labourers' Act, the regulations, and the instructions were all so perfect and elaborate that people wondered how it was that illegal acts could be done. He had no hesitation whatsoever in pronouncing the labour traffic so inherently bad that it could not be regulated.

VITAL STATISTICS.

The vital statistics for 1892 showed that the death rate for Queensland was 12.06 to 1000 of the population, leaving out Chinese, Polynesians, and all other alien races. But the death rate per 1000 of the Polynesian population in Queensland was 42.74, in round numbers 43 in 1000 blacks, to 12 per 1000 whites. In 1892 and 1893, the death of Polynesians was 709. Information supplied by the department showed that 49,009 Kanakas had been brought to Queensland between 1888 and 1893, and of that number, he estimated, 11,000 had died.

MR. GRAY'S INDICTMENT.

His indictment against the traffic was as follows: 1. It demoralises and impoverishes the Kanaka, deprives him of his citizenship, and depopulates the islands. 2. The regulations under which it exists in Queensland are inadequate to prevent abuses, and in the nature of the case, they cannot be anything else. 3. The whole thing is contrary to the spirit of the Gospel. That spirit is that the strong should help the weak. But the Kanaka is trodden down. He is the man who went down to Jericho and fell among thieves.

THE REV. MR. SMITH IN REPLY.

In the first place, Mr. Gray had given them a good deal of information, and in the second place, he had spoken on the whole temperately. Of course, they knew that looking at it from a missionary point of view, Mr. Gray must feel somewhat sore on certain points. He (Mr. Smith) would like to refer to what had been said about the mortality among the Kanakas. About four years ago, the mortality was about 98 out of 3000. Since then, the rate has steadily diminished, until last year it was reduced to 25 or 30 in the thousand. He thought that if the Kanakas were so ill-used as he said they were when they were brought here; it was a remarkable thing that out of the thousands employed in the Mackay district there were very few who had not been from three to fifteen years in the colony, and they would not go home. As to wages, Mr. Gray said they got about £9 a year. Perhaps he was not aware that under the restrictions placed on the Kanaka traffic, labour had become somewhat scarce and the result had been in the Mackay district that the larger proportion of 2000 Kanakas got from £20 to £40 a year. He wished they could say that every white man was as well paid, as well fed, and as well treated as those Kanakas were. (Applause.)[139]

THE SUGAR INDUSTRY — REVIEW OF THE YEAR 1897. BEET AND CANE SUGAR THROUGHOUT THE WORLD — QUEENSLAND.

Queensland was a peculiarly interesting country to cane sugar producers, inasmuch as the various problems connected with cultivation, manufacture, labour, and the intelligent encouragement of the industry by Government support had found a solution in that colony which had not been possible elsewhere to anything like the same extent. It was calculated that over one-fourth of the cultivated land was occupied by cane, and as the franchise was on a broad basis, and the general standard of intelligence and education was tolerably high, the growers and manufacturers of cane sugar were able to make their influence felt in a forcible and effectual manner than was possible in other countries growing sugar. Under the Acts in force, as soon as an adequate supply of cane could be insured by the farmers of any district, the erection of a central factory could be secured by the Government advancing capital. This system promoted the prosperity of the sugar industry to such an extent that the colony produced nearly the whole of the sugar required by itself and the neighbouring colonies of Australasia, and with the prospect to export to Great Britain or elsewhere. The greatest difficulty had been the supply at a reasonable cost of reliable labour adapted to the tropical climate. This was secured by the Legislature permitting the introduction of Kanakas (South Sea Islanders),

---

139 Brisbane Courier 8 February 1895 p 6, abridged.

but now that the question of Australian federation was to the fore it was again constituting a difficulty, as the whites in the neighbouring colonies did not view with any satisfaction the employment of any but white labour, which had hitherto proved unreliable, as well as excessively costly. A further difficulty was the question of levying an extra countervailing duty on bounty-fed foreign sugars, in view of the fact that the competition of German beet sugar in the southern markets of Australia was becoming troublesome. This would not accord with the free-trade policy of New South Wales. These questions, connected with possible federation and the way in which the claims of the Queensland sugar producers could be met, were only in a nascent state. One thing seemed certain, without Kanaka labour, the production of sugar in Queensland at present prices could not be maintained. The number of Kanakas was about 8000. The annual production of Queensland was about 100,000 tons, the home consumption being about one-fourth. It appeared not unlikely that Queensland would also have to face the competition of Australian-grown beet sugar, as experiments on a fairly extensive scale were going on at Maffra (Victoria) and Tenterfield (New South Wales).[140]

PACIFIC ISLAND LABOURERS ACT 1901.

The Pacific Island Labourers Act 1901 (Cth) was enacted by the Parliament of Australia to facilitate the deportation of Pacific Islanders, or Kanakas working in the Queensland sugar industry. [Assented to 17 December 1901.] With the enactment of the Immigration Restriction Act 1901(Cth), the White Australia policy was implemented:

> 3. No Pacific Island labourer shall enter Australia on or

---

140 Brisbane Courier 18 February 1898 p 7, abridged.

after the thirty-first day of March, One thousand nine hundred and four.

2

Assessment

This book relates to marine incidents under the jurisdiction of the colony of Queensland involving indigenous Pacific Islanders also known as South Sea Islanders. Set out in Table A are a series of marine incidents that meet the criteria of a Queensland connection and South Sea Islander presence. There were 149 incidents, which might be tabulated and analysed under the following headings: judicial trial or administrative inquiry, Royal Navy intervention, wrecks, attacks on boat crews, and attacks on ships. The total number of islander deaths and the number of deaths of white men are also set out in the table below. These mortality figures include deaths from shipwrecks (drowning) and killings from collisions between whites and islanders.

The data does not include deaths from diseases, illnesses or medical conditions. The short answer for the exclusion of that data is this. With the benefit of hindsight, it is now known that South Sea Islanders had not acquired immunity to certain common diseases then prevalent amongst white populations.[141]

---

141 Infectious diseases, including smallpox, bubonic plague, chickenpox, cholera, the common cold, diphtheria, influenza, malaria, measles, scarlet fever, sexually transmitted diseases, typhoid, typhus, dysentery, and tuberculosis.

On exposure to these diseases, the islanders naturally fell victim to the pathogen and died. Since this was a phenomenon occurring worldwide during the nineteenth century and earlier, concerning uncontacted indigenous populations and that medical science at the time was unaware of such issues, I do not consider it a factor capable of colonial governance.[142] To a commentator of the twenty-first century, it is abundantly clear that if people are concentrated for whatever reason, even a benign ocean cruise and proper standards of hygiene and sanitation are not provided and, more importantly, not supervised or enforced, water and food will be contaminated and diseases such as dysentery, typhoid and diarrhoea will spread with ease and the death rate will climb drastically.[143]

MARINE INCIDENTS BY TYPE

Trial, Inquiry	RN Intervention	Wrecks	Attacks on boat crews	Attacks on ships	SSI deaths	white men deaths
55	42	34	54	5	316	58

For these marine incidents to have any meaning, the data needs to be put against the background of the overall shipping activity in the area of study. Each year, the Queensland government published the Statistics of the Colony of Queensland. The Immigration Department provided for the publication, a table of Polynesian Immigration and a table of Polynesian Emigration. These yearly tables provided the source material for the identification of vessels, labour vessel traffic and yearly total

---

142 The Black Armband Brigade in Australia take the opposite view and hold the colonial governments responsible for the deaths of the islanders by disease. Saunders, 1974:293; 1982:89-91.

143 The high mortality rates among immigrant labourers related to their lack of immunity to diseases, not to lack of food or to substantial physical mistreatment (Shlomowitz 1987, 1989). Revising the Revisionists: The Historiography of Immigrant Melanesians in Australia, Clive Moore, June 1992 p 65.

adult labour returnees and adult labour recruits.[144] There were 816 outward-bound journeys with returnees and 784 inward journeys with recruits, for the period 1868 to 1905, a total of 1600 journeys.[145]

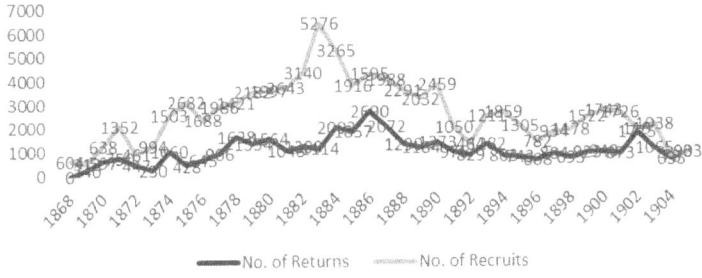

---

[144] The reader is referred to the annual Votes and Proceedings of the Queensland Legislative Assembly publication.

[145] See page 213 below.

For the Period 1868-1905

Journeys	No. of SSI Returnees[146]	No. of SSI Recruits	Average No. per trip
Out 816	39661		1071.91
In 784		59434	1606.32
Total 1600			

The 55 incidents under the heading Trial/Inquiry may be broken down further. Courts of law and administrative or ministerial inquiries have been traditionally viewed as two distinct and separate groups. Administrative inquiries are concerned with government issues within the framework of ministerial responsibilities, such as adherence to government policy, bureaucratic rules and procedures, suitability and conduct of appointees and office holders, observance of financial and budgetary regulations and directions, etc.

Court of Law		Administrative Inquiry	
Slavery	2	Royal Com	8
Kidnapping	11	Boards	16
W/O licence	5		
Criminal	13		

The cases of slavery arose out of the seizure by Captain Palmer of *H.M.S. Rosario*, of the schooner *Daphne* for a breach of the Slave Trade Act (Imp.) The owners of the vessel Daggett and Pritchard were brought up before the Water Police court at Sydney on a charge of slavery but the charge was dismissed for want of evidence. The schooner *Daphne* was suited for condemnation and forfeiture as a slaver in the Vice-Admiralty Court at Sydney. After a lengthy judgment, the court held that the Slave Act applied in African and American waters but not in South Pacific seas where free native labourers were carried.

---

146 Please note that in 1906, 2,438 SSI were returned and in 1907 a further 3,278 SSI were returned, see p 213 below.

Eleven cases of kidnapping were brought before the courts.[147] All, except Delargy and Coath, were prosecuted under the Imperial Kidnapping Acts of 1872 and 1875. Convictions were obtained in Coath of the *Jason*, 5 years' jail;[148] McLean and Rowen of the *Forest King*, 3 years' jail with the first year in irons for each prisoner; Mills and Burton of the *Ethel*, 7 years and 2 years with the first in irons, respectively; and Shaw, Schofield, Freeman, Rogers and Preston of the *Hopeful*, life with 3 years in irons, life with 3 years in irons, 10 years with 2 years irons, 7 years with 1 year in irons, 7 years with 1 year in irons, respectively. The cases in which the Crown failed to obtain a conviction for kidnapping were: *Active, May Queen, Jessie Kelley, Forest King* (Owners), *Ethel* (Loutit), *Stanley* and *Voss*.

The case of R v Coath (labour vessel *Jason*) has been of interest to past commentators. Captain Coath was prosecuted under the common law of England, as his case occurred before the enactment of the Imperial Kidnapping Act of 1872.[149] He was convicted of kidnapping nine islanders in February 1871. On appeal, Mr Lilley, for the appellant, argued from a basis of first principles given that the matter involved the common law of England:

> Can it (kidnapping) be committed on a savage or barbarous people captured and brought within the protection of British law, and landed free at Maryborough? The offence of kidnapping only arises where persons are taken from under the protection of the law of England, where the Sovereign is deprived of a

---

147 Clive Moore included the *Lady Darling* in 1875, the *Jabberwock* in 1881 and the *Heron* in 1883. I have excluded them because I don't consider his sources are of substantial probative value; Moore, Clive (1981) Kanaka Maratta: a history of Melanesian Mackay. PhD thesis, James Cook University, pp 83-89.

148 Was pardoned in 1873.

149 Slaving in Australian Courts: Blackbirding Cases, 1869-1871, Reid Mortensen, Journal of South Pacific Law, Vol. 4, 2000.

subject, or where there is concealment of a person in any part of the British dominions so as to deprive the person of the protection of the laws. Under Roman law, it was no offence to steal or capture barbarous people, and the offence only existed where a freeman, his wife or child, was seized and held as a slave. It is no offence to go to islands inhabited by a savage and barbarous people and to bring these people within the protection of the English law.

The appeal court dismissed the appeal and said:

> And yet men are found to sail forth from a port of this colony and seize and carry away certain persons found on the high seas—they are called islanders, and whether they are civilised or not, matters not. They have a right to liberty, which is inherent in all human beings, although at times that inherent right has been taken away by force. But we have nothing to do with that; we must assume that at the time these men were taken they were freemen, and that being so it is an offence on the high seas by persons subject to the jurisdiction of the British Courts.

The *Stanley* also offered an interesting case, on 3 April 1884, at the City Police Court, Brisbane, Captain Joseph Griffiths Davies and William A McMurdo were charged on the information of Charles Colville Horrocks, acting Immigration Agent with having, on or about 17 April 1883 being then on the high seas near the Laughlan Islands of kidnapping two islanders named Sea Whimp and Na Mee. In the course of these proceedings, Davies and McMurdo were arrested on warrants issued by the High Commissioner for the Western Pacific, which resulted in the defendants remanded into prison pending their removal to Fiji, to be dealt with by the High Commissioner of the Western Pacific. As a consequence of the removal of the defendants out of the jurisdiction of Queensland, the kidnapping charge was withdrawn. On 20 December 1884, Lord Derby, Secretary of State for the Colonies, advised Governor Musgrave that he was satisfied by the action taken in the *Stanley* case. The upshot of this matter was that Davies and McMurdo were tried on (1) having set fire to a storehouse and dwelling house; (2) having burnt the dwelling houses of certain natives; and (3) having destroyed property of the natives not exceeding the value of £5.

The constant refrain of blackbirding kanakas for the cane fields of Queensland does not seem to be supported by the evidence. Yet it remains engraved on the minds of certain sections of the Australian community, like the mark of Cain.[150]

The next group of cases involved carrying, without a licence, native labourers of the islands of the Pacific Ocean. The cases were prosecuted under the provisions of the Kidnapping Acts of 1872 and 1875. On the enactment of the Kidnapping Act of 1872, the Royal Navy issued instructions for the guidance of commanders of Her Majesty's ships of war employed in the suppression of the kidnapping trade.[151] Armed with the instructions and her sailing directions, *H.M.S. Basilisk* proceeded north from Sydney to the fishing ground of north Queensland and the Torres Strait and intercepted *Woodbine*, *Crishna*, *Melanie*, *Challenge*, and *Aurora*. On 9 January 1873, the barque *Woodbine* was boarded. Finding that the ship had no articles and three South Sea Islanders onboard without a licence and that the master could give no explanation, the vessel was sent to Brisbane in charge of Lieutenant S. G. Smith, where she was eventually released for want of sufficient evidence.[152] *Crishna* is an interesting case. Captain Walton entered into a

---

150 Revisionism and Its Enemies: Debating the Queensland Labour Trade, Doug Munro, The Journal of Pacific History, Dec., 1995, Vol. 30, No. 2 (Dec., 1995), pp. 240-249. Docker, The Blackbirders, 1970 is a good example of fake history.

151 http://nla.gov.au/nla.obj-1480637885

152 New Guinea & Polynesia. Discoveries & surveys in New Guinea and the D'Entrecasteaux Islands; a cruise in Polynesia and visits to the pearl-shelling stations in Torres Straits of H. M. S. Basilisk by Moresby, John, London, J. Murray 1876 p 124. Note: not included in above data; mentioned in the interest of completeness.

contract to carry the passengers and cargo of Captain Delargy, of the *Active*. Some of the passengers were from the Pacific Islands. Walton appeared to have ignored the provisions of the Kidnapping Act of 1872. As a result, the *Crishna* and her cargo were condemned and forfeited to the Crown. The Crown on auctioning the ship and cargo realised £4000. The owners were quick to claim on their insurance policy with the Australian Insurance Company on the ground that Walton had been guilty of barratry. The Australian Insurance Company refused to pay, and the matter was finally determined in the Privy Council, which delivered judgment on 29 June 1875 and dismissed the appeal of the Australasian Insurance Company with costs. This whole episode of the *Basilisk* had the effect of driving South Sea Islanders out of the pearl shelling and bêche-de-mer fishing in north Queensland and the Torres Strait.[153]

In the cases of *Melanie* and *Challenge*, the court expressed the view that although the case had been proved "to enforce the forfeiture, in a case of this kind would be harsh in the highest degree". The Crown in each case, therefore, consented to give up the vessel and release the bond, provided the respondents bear their costs of the defence and their costs of the appeal, and withdraw the notice of the appeal. Finally, in the case of the *Aurora*, the court found a loophole in the Kidnapping Act. *H.M.S. Sandfly* had intercepted *Aurora* and seized her under the act, but proceeded against the cargo of the vessel and not the ship itself. The court held it had no power to condemn and order forfeiture of the cargo. Perhaps one can infer that the courts viewed the penalty for carrying natives without a licence, as a draconian punishment, which it was, the forfeiture of a ship and cargo, and therefore, sought to soften the penalties where they could. The last case in the series was the *Margaret and Jane*.

---

[153] See *Bêche-de-mer and the Binghis* by Paul Dillon and *Dispela Kantri Belong Mi, Nau!* by Paul Dillon.

Here again, the matter fizzled out. The native, the subject of the carrying, was found to be a stowaway. The Crown withdrew the prosecution on the defence paying the cost of the seizure and prosecution.

These carrying cases caused great consternation among the mercantile community of Sydney. So much so that the shipowners convened a meeting over the matter and wrote to Commodore Goodenough of the Australian Station:

Shipowners

Sydney, 15 August 1874

Re: Kidnapping Act

> For upwards of 70 years a considerable trade has been carried on from this port to the South Sea Islands and from the nature of the trade the aid of the Islanders was invariably resorted to and in fact, it could not be carried on without island labour and the islanders so employed were for all practical purposes considered and treated as part of the crew of the vessels engaged in the trade and this view was born out by the provisions of the Merchant Shipping Act of 1854. The Act thus recognised as part of the crew, men, who should not be sailors but engaged in any capacity onboard a ship.
>
> When the Kidnapping Act was passed enacting "that it shall not be lawful for any British ship to carry native labourers of the said islands not being part of the crew of the said ship" it was never dreamt of by shipowners that such a restriction should apply to men who for years had formed an indispensable part of the ship's crew when engaged in the South Sea Island trade.
>
> The offences against which the Kidnapping Act was intended to provide are enumerated in clause 9 of the Act and I venture to say that in no single instance where a vessel has been condemned in this colony or Queensland under this Act were any of the offences enumerated proved, but in every instance, the condemnation was decried on the ground that the ship carried

"native labourers" without a licence in violation of the 6th clause. The term native labourer was thus made to extend to the class of men who for so many years had been regarded as part of the crew and whom the Merchant Shipping Act warranted shipowners in regarding as part of their crew.

In no single instance brought before the Supreme Court of this colony was any outrage or act of barbarity ever alleged against any of the vessels seized under the Kidnapping Act while engaged in the South Sea Island trade. If the Act had been construed and carried out in the light of Lord Kimberley's circular dispatch accompanying the Act, no such seizures or condemnations could have taken place. In the 3rd clause of that despatch he, in express terms, alludes to the benefits derived by the natives from a properly regulated intercourse with Europeans and is careful to provide that the natives and their employers should not be deprived of such benefits arising from the only intercourse of which he was aware, viz. the emigration of natives to other than their native islands.

The shipowners of this port have reason to believe that you are willing when application is made to you to grant to shipmasters proceeding on such voyages a letter to protect them from seizure by any British vessels as long as no abuse is made of the privilege. George R. Dibbs, Shipowners.

18 July 1874

George Dibbs

Ship Owners

Sydney

You are doubtless aware that although I am instructed generally to afford all aid in my power to lawful commerce; yet my particular duty with reference to the employment of native labourers is to take care that the provisions of the Kidnapping Act 1872 are strictly complied with according to the true meaning and intention of that Act which was to secure natives from any sort of ill-treatment or compulsion on the part of British subjects.

I should therefore inform you to prevent application being made to me on mistaken grounds that although in the exercise of any discretion, I have given such directions to the officers commanding Her Majesty's cruisers as will secure lawful traders from interference on account of the want of a licence which they are unable to obtain under the provisions of the Act yet that I have not and cannot give special protection to any particular vessel by letter or otherwise. Such protection could only be given by the authority of Her Majesty's government, through the officer of the port from which such a vessel sails and, after survey of that vessel and an engagement on the part of her owners and master.

I should also inform you that under this Act any vessel is still liable to seizure which carries native labourers without a licence, and will be detained if it should appear that the natives employed onboard her are in any way ill-treated, overcrowded, embarked or detained against their will or set onshore against their will at any other than their island and district. Goodenough, Australian Station.[154]

The criminal matters involved murder and a string of other crimes of violence. The murder convictions arose in the *Alfred Vittery*. Captain Boore, Freeman, government agent and 4 white crew members were charged with the murder of two South Sea Islanders on 4 October 1883 while on the high seas. The evidence was confusing; it appeared that two recruits became uncontrollable. They were fired on and their bodies were then thrown overboard. In the process, one of the recruits was said to be still alive, and Grimes finished him off. The jury convicted Grimes of manslaughter and recommended him to mercy. The others were found not guilty. Grimes was discharged on his own recognisance.

The next case was the *Hopeful*, McNeil and Williams were each convicted of the murder of a South Sea Islander and sentenced to

---

154 http://nla.gov.au/nla.obj-1470773241 (images 99-111, file 6304).

death. On 24 December 1884, their sentence was commuted to life imprisonment with the first five years in irons. The Executive released all the *Hopeful* prisoners on 19 February 1890.

The next case is that of the *Douro*. Captain Sorensen proved to be a reprobate of the worst type. His honour said:

> You began your voyage by an act of lawlessness, in which you violated the principles of Imperial law. You attempted to conceal the character of your vessel in order that you might prosecute your trade without being compelled to submit to the obligation of British law. The offence committed off Carpenter Island, if it did not amount to the crime of piracy, undoubtedly contained many elements of that offence. It is an offence regarded as of the highest gravity by the British law, and the punishment is the highest known to the law short of death. The committal of a crime of this description does not unfortunately terminate with the completion of the crime itself. It reacts upon innocent victims. Persons visiting these islands for the purposes of honest trade are likely after such acts of violence to meet with a revengeful and hostile display on the part of the islanders when they come in contact with them.

Turning now to the sub-group entitled, Administrative Inquiry, the first category relates to the Royal Commission appointed on 23 December 1884, to inquire into the circumstances under which divers labourers, natives of New Guinea and other islands in the Western Pacific were recruited. The inquiry found that the ships *Ceara, Lizzie, Hopeful, Forest King, Heath,* and *Sybil* had in the course of recruiting in the specified locations under investigation seduced islanders on board by false pretences; as a consequence, the government returned the recruits to their homelands. What is of interest here is that proceedings were only commenced against the ships' crew of the *Hopeful*, arising out of the findings of the Royal Commission.[155] The Royal

---

155 Wawn, 1893, p 368.

Commission noted as follows:

> Wherever there was pronounced unwillingness on the part of natives to go in the boats or remain in the ships they were too often impressed by threats, though cases of overt kidnapping were confined almost wholly to one voyage— viz., to that of the *Hopeful*—as was also the dastardly act of wrecking canoes and driving the occupants into the water that they might be rescued by the ship's boats.[156]

The next category in this sub-group relates to Immigration and or Marine Board Inquiries of which 16 were identified.[157] Eight Immigration inquiries led to captains being debarred from labour vessels on seven occasions, and one occasion where the actions of the G.A. were justified. Eight Marine Inquiries resulted in captains being exonerated on 3 occasions, censured in one incident, a master's certificate cancelled, a master's certificate suspended for 6 months in another, and a mate found responsible for the foundering of a ship.

The data also revealed that the Royal Navy involved itself in the labour trade between Queensland and the South Pacific. The presence of the Royal Navy need hardly be commented on. After all, its greatest captain discovered Australia, and it was present at the birth of the country. I could have perhaps selected any starting place in the history of the Royal Navy's presence in the South Pacific. However, for the want of a better place to start, the reader is directed to Captain Erskine's (*H.M.S. Havannah*) report dated 10 October 1849, Proceedings at the South Sea Islands:

> I take the liberty of calling their Lordships' attention to that on the New Hebrides, New Caledonia, and the Loyalty Islands, places little known, except by the sandalwood

---

156 Qld Parl. V & P 1885 Vol. II p 797ff, p xix.

157 The author acknowledges that further Immigration and or Marine Board Inquiries may be identified.

traders, but which from their proximity to our Australian colonies, the nature of the trade carried on with them, and the consequences likely to ensue, appear to require more immediate attention than any of the other islands in this part of the Pacific.[158]

If one treats this statement by Erskine as a policy statement of interest and intent, it is clear that the Royal Navy had a substantial commitment in the South Pacific, particularly, in trade and mercantile activities. As the market moved from harvesting sandalwood to the recruitment and transportation of labour from the South Pacific, so did the focus of the Royal Navy. In 1868, Palmer of *H.M.S. Rosario* intercepted a vessel, *Daphne*, acting suspiciously in transporting natives from one island to another. He assessed the situation and formed the view that the conduct and manner of carrying passengers suggested the vessel was a slaver. He seized the vessel and then brought proceedings in Sydney before the Vice-Admiralty Court for condemnation and forfeiture of the vessel. He failed.

The development of the labour trade in the South Sea Islands began to alarm certain sections of the UK and colonial communities. By the time the labour trade had established itself, there was a substantial British missionary presence in the South Pacific. The missionaries motivated by Christian principles opposed this trade and lobbied the UK government to have it banned. The UK Government agreed to intervene but only to control and regulate the trade, not to ban it outright. As a consequence, the Imperial Kidnapping Act of 1872 was enacted. This act created several statutory offences which were enforced by the Royal Navy. The 1872 Act was enlarged by the Imperial amending act of 1875 and extended the jurisdiction to a geographical area known as the Western Pacific. In 1877,

---

158 http://nla.gov.au/nla.obj-1430837490 Capt. Erskine Reporting Proceedings at the South Sea Islands, images 3-12, file 5606.

the British government formalised and promulgated the powers and administrative provisions of the High Commissioner for the Western Pacific by the Western Pacific Order-in-Council.[159]

The Royal Navy continued its operations from the Australian Station at Sydney over the South Sea Islands. These patrols, among other matters, involved the Royal Navy responding to calls for assistance from British subjects either living or voyaging in the South Sea Islands and other foreign nationals.[160] In May 1877, Commodore Hoskins, Australian Station was informed that Easterbrook, a British subject at Tanna Island had been murdered by natives. Hoskins directed Lieut. Caffin of *H.M.S. Beagle* to proceed to Tanna and investigate the murder and:

> should you be fully convinced that it was not his own misconduct which led to the commission of the deed, you are, should you deem your force sufficient, to endeavour to obtain possession of the murderer; and, if successful, you are to cause him to be executed in the most public and judicial manner possible.

Lieut. Caffin duly carried out his orders and held an inquiry that found Nokwai, a Tanese, guilty of the murder of Easterbrook. At 10 am on 25 September 1877, Nokwai was hung from the foreyard arm of *H.M.S. Beagle* until dead. At 2 pm the body was taken down and buried.[161]

The Secretary of the Admiralty advised Commodore Hoskins as follows:

> My Lords, in conclusion, desire me to state that they cannot impress upon you too strongly the necessity of exercising the greatest caution in dealing with the natives. The officers employed on such service should strictly observe the special directions

---

159 See page 78 above.
160 See pages 88-91 above (Gordon's letter).
161 http://nla.gov.au/nla.obj-1353957842 (images 147 to 153, file 6453); HC paper 65.

contained in the Instructions of 1873 for the suppression of the kidnapping trade, bearing in mind that it is their duty alike to protect British subjects from the unprovoked attack of savages, and the natives from the lawless acts of white men, and in directing your particular attention to the provisions of the Pacific Islanders Protection Act, and to the Order-in-Council under it, which were sent to you in my letter of 8th January last, my Lords feel assured that whenever it is possible to do so, you will leave any offences which can be dealt with by the High Commissioner or his deputy, to be adjudicated by those officers.[162]

The actions of *H.M.S. Basilisk* demonstrated the enforcement powers of the Royal Navy. But it was destructive of the pearl shell and bêche-de-mer fisheries in Queensland. NSW boats left Queensland waters and kanakas could no longer be employed in those industries in Queensland waters. Many of the instances where the Royal Navy was shown to have intervened were post facto sanctions against the indigenous islanders, as in the case of the murder of the boat's crew of the *Mystery* at Aoba Island in 1877. *H.M.S. Wolverine*, unlike in the case of Easterbrook, landed a large contingent of bluejackets and forced the offending tribe to hand over the principal offender, who was then taken prisoner and transferred to Fiji. In the case of the *May Queen* incident of 1878, *H.M.S. Beagle*, Commander De Houghton, organised an expedition against the natives, being assisted by twenty Solomon Islanders, besides Captain Satina, the second officer, and the Government agent (Mr. Lynde), all of whom volunteered from the *Sybil*. The natives escaped into the surrounding bush; consequently, their village was burned down.

By 30 March 1882, the sailing orders given by the Officer Commanding the Australian Station were as follows:

Commodore Erskine to Lieutenant Maturin, *H.M.S.*

---

[162] http://nla.gov.au/nla.obj-1353997373 (images 225 to 230, file 6453); HC paper 223.

Beagle.

4. Much tact and discretion is necessary in all dealings with the natives of these groups, as also when called upon to settle disputes which frequently arise between them and resident traders. It will be your endeavour to carry out a firm but conciliatory policy towards those with whom you are brought in contact; and should you investigate a case of massacre on the part of the native, you are to bear in mind that, having no jurisdiction over these people, you can only proceed against them, their guilt being clearly established, by an Act of War, which is not to be lightly undertaken, and in no case indiscriminate slaughter of natives, or wanton destruction of fruit-trees, to be permitted.[163]

In the case of the murder of Captain Belbin, *H.M.S. Dart's* actions of killing eight islanders and levying a fine on the villagers were approved by the Foreign Office. Then there were the actions of *H.M.S. Diamond* against the villagers of Marati over the *Lavinia* incident of 1883; *H.M.S. Miranda* and the *Flora* incident of 1884; also *H.M.S. Opal* and the *Young Dick* incident of 1886. The actions of the Royal Navy in the matter of the murder of Armstrong of the *Ariel* by shelling the offending village demonstrated the limitations of the Navy in bringing islanders to book.

The labour vessel *May*, in 1890, was alleged to have illegally recruited labourers by *H.M.S. Royalist*. After a searching inquiry by the Queensland government, Mr. Griffith advised:

> This Government has always gratefully recognised the assistance of the commanders of Her Majesty's ships in the Pacific in supervising the recruiting trade, and have always, I believe, cheerfully endorsed any action taken by them within the scope of their instructions upon the subject. But in the present instance, I desire to point out that the

---

163 http://nla.gov.au/nla.obj-1374760020 (image 179, file 6675).

evidence before Captain Davis was entirely hearsay, and was not corroborated by any sworn testimony.

Finally, within this group, is the case of the death of Bergin, *Rio Loge*, 1896, which was investigated by Commander Adams, *H.M.S. Pylades*, at Auki, 18 June 1896. He found no fault with the natives, as the fire was in self-defence.

The next group of significance is Wrecks. Thirty-four wrecks were recorded. In the majority of cases, the crew and the passengers (recruits/returnees) were saved.

Wrecks involving loss of life

Vessel	South Sea Islanders lost	Whites lost
Reliance	70	4
Noumea	7	
Fredericka Wilhelmina	1	3
Young Dick	117	3
Sybil	3	
Northern Belle	16	4
Liza Mary	46	5
Total deaths	260	19

From thirty-four wrecks a total of 279 crew and passengers lost their lives, presumably by drowning. Furthermore, the data revealed that on 4 occasions, the wrecks were plundered by the indigenous natives domiciled at the place of the wreck. The study has not sought to examine the extent or monetary value of the property damage caused by the loss of a vessel and or the contents of a vessel, nor has the study sought to establish the cause of the loss of a vessel.[164] These figures seem remarkably low when put alongside the number of trips made to the South Seas, 1600 in total. That is 2.125% of the shipping traffic of labour vessels.

---

164 Where an inquiry made a finding, I noted the outcome of the inquiry.

ASSESSMENT

Table 1[165]

LOCATION & FREQUENCY OF LABOUR VESSELS ATTACKED 1868-1905

Location	Frequency
Ambry Is.	4 / 7
Aurora Is.	1
Buka	1
Cape Pitt	1
Erroma	1
Fatuna Is.	2 / 3
Hogg	1
Malaita	1
Malo Is.	1 / 11 / 8
Moona	2
Pau-	1
Qui Is.	1 / 2 / 5
Santa	3
Tongoa Is.	1 / 1 / 7 / 5
Vale Is.	3 / 2 / 1 / 1

Table 2

ATTACKS ON LABOUR SHIPS & CREWS 1869-1901

Year	Attacks
1869	1
1870	0
1871	3
1872	1
1873	2 / 3
1874	0
1875	1
1876	0
1877	4
1878	1
1879	2
1880	0
1881	6 / 5
1882	1
1883	9
1884	3
1885	3
1886	0
1887	1
1888	1
1889	1
1890	2
1891	4 / 1
1892	0
1893	0
1894	0
1895	2
1896	0
1897	0
1898	2
1899	0
1901	0

---

165 Table 1 & 2 show a representation of Locations and Vessels from the data collected; refer to pp 202-212 below.

The final group is the Attacks on Boat Crews and Ships. By and large, these attacks caused the wounding and/or deaths of the two principal groups, South Sea Islanders and whites.[166] There were 54 attacks on boat crews while recruiting and 5 attacks on ships.[167] The loss of life under these headings was for islanders 56 and whites 39. All the deaths of the whites were at the hands of islanders except in the case of the *Ariel* where the death was by suicide and in the case of the *May Queen* where the death was by drowning. Not all the deaths of the islanders were at the hands of whites. The manning of boat crews consisted of islander oarsmen and one or two white men. Of the 54 attacks on boat crews, the attacks commenced with the islanders using traditional weapons such as bows and arrows, spears, and tomahawks. However, once the islanders obtained firearms, the modus operandi was to fire on boat crews attempting to recruit in the vicinity of their village. On occasions, islander boat crew were wounded or killed along with the whites in the boat. The loss of life from collisions between labour vessels(whites) and islanders again appears very low given the total number of trips, at 3.56%. The source material suggests that the marksmanship of the islanders was very poor and accounts for their lack of effective firepower. Of course, if the inward recruiting trips are used as a base, it would be 7.27% of the inward labour traffic, still a low incidence of attack.

Captain C Bridge, *H.M.S. Espiègle*, in his report to the High Commissioner for the Western Pacific of 27 July 1882, observed:

---

166 Whites may be a coarse term but there is no other suitable word available to my mind. European or Caucasian does not fit the bill as it is not important where they came from; it is simply a matter of fact; white men owned and operated the vessels.

167 Not all incidents of firing on boats have been identified. The number of incidents would therefore be in excess of the recorded number of 53, see annual Pacific Island Immigration Reports.

8. That class of outrage by the inhabitants which consists of firing on boats' crews is, if accounts may be believed, far from uncommon. Without firearms, such things could not happen. A respectable and experienced captain of a labour vessel informed me that he was of the opinion that this firing was often nothing more than a heedless freak of some savage just gratified by becoming the owner of a gun. He compared it to the use of the catapult by schoolboys in England. The whole metropolitan police have been unable to suppress the use of the catapult in London, and the suppression of the use of firearms in these islands by any force likely to be employed amongst them is altogether impossible. Outrages of this kind must therefore go on as long as the means of perpetrating them are available.[168]

Lieutenant-Commander Moore, *H.M.S. Dart*, 13 August 1883 to Commodore Erskine reported as follows:

Moreover, this tribe (Ballab), the worst no doubt in Ambrym, is only one of many that make it a practice to fire on labour vessels and their boats when opportunities present themselves.

14. It must also be well known that many of the tribes are armed with Snider rifles, which they buy in or receive from Queensland, and that shooting at boats is common.

15. Firing at boats is indeed so usual that it would not be possible for one ship in this group to take serious notice of half the cases that occur—she can only act on some aggravated instance, to make an example. Here was such a case: The small tribe of Ballab, perhaps not numbering more than fifty fighting men, waging a sort of war on white men and firing off a very considerable amount of ammunition at everybody who happened to come that way for twelve months.[169]

Although there were only five attacks on ships, they were serious. The first ship attacked was the *Janet Stewart* on 12 February

---

168 http://nla.gov.au/nla.obj-1359444845 (image 312, file 6623).
169 http://nla.gov.au/nla.obj-1375391192 (image 807, file 6676).

1882 at Malaita Island. The captain and second mate went off recruiting in two boats and left six crew and the government agent onboard with a number of recruits. Natives came off the island and boarded the ship, killing five crew members and the government agent. Only one crew member survived. The Royal Navy investigated the matter and consequently punished the natives by destroying their village and cutting down a portion of their coconut trees. While the *Helena's* boats were away recruiting, a number of Tongoa islanders boarded the schooner and incited the recruits to seize the ship. The boats shortly afterwards returned, and a serious conflict ensued. The mutiny was eventually quelled with three of the natives killed. The next incident involved the *Emily*. On 18 December 1884, the brig *Emily* was anchored in Hogg Harbour, Espiritu Santo Island, about 150 yards from the shore. While the crew and recruits were at dinner on deck, and without any warning or provocation whatever, they were fired on by the natives on shore. Fortunately, no one on board was injured.

The attack on the schooner *Elibank Castle* at the Solomon Islands on 17 or 18 May 1885, in which the captain and all hands, except David Brown, were massacred could not be corroborated by the Royal Navy. The final incident involved the *Young Dick*. Four white men were killed, and seventeen natives were killed by the surviving white crew in defending the ship.

On 3 July 1886, G. Tryon, Commander-in-Chief, Australian Station wrote to J. B. Thurston concerning attacks by natives on the labour schooner *Young Dick* in May 1886 at Malaita:

> 7. No precautions were taken by those left on board; on the contrary, the natives, who were so greatly distrusted by those in the boats, were freely admitted on board. It may have been that the trade gear exposed to view awakened the cupidity of

the natives. Whatever was the cause, an opportunity was rashly and most imprudently offered to men of the same race, living on the same island, who on two previous occasions within but a few days interval had, it is represented, treacherously assaulted a portion of the crew.

13. (Should) a man-of-war be placed in a position to which they should not be exposed without strong reason. Does it exist in this case, in which by reason of rashness and incaution, to say the least, white men in pursuit of gain have taken their lives in their own hands, and have placed themselves unarmed in the power of natives, known to be treacherous and evil-disposed, and whose ways we, so far, have not mended?

14. On the other hand, it may he held that it is not unlawful to engage in "labour" trade, and men employed on what is lawful, and among savages, should be protected, or allowed to take the law into their own hands; this latter is quite inadmissible; the argument cannot apply beyond certain limits. We can only proceed by act of war, and that within certain restrictions, such as may be described as taking punitive measures.

15. In this instance the natives must feel they suffered severely at the hands of two courageous white men. They obtained no plunder. They, and those who hear of it, will hesitate before they endeavour to plunder a vessel, and vessels will read the lesson that it is right to themselves and right to the natives to take proper precautions.

16. Should I hereafter determine to send a vessel with the view, if possible, and without undue risk, to punish the offending natives, and if it is not found reasonably practicable to do so, will more harm than good arise?[170]

The level of incidents when put against the shipping traffic of 1600 passages over the period 1868 to 1905, in conjunction with the level of technology available at the time, in my view,

---

170 Papers relating to the recent Operations of H.M.S. OPAL against Natives of the Solomon Islands. House of Commons, 11 February 1887, 58 p 16.

seems remarkably low. Furthermore, I find it difficult to identify a specific government policy of discrimination. South Sea Islanders were guest workers who required different ethical considerations.[171]

---

171 The features of guest worker schemes vary, but most restrict the rights of migrants to settle permanently; to move freely between different employers; and migrant workers' residency rights are conditional upon retaining employment with their sponsoring employer.

3

Compare and Contrast

Taking the three groups together, the statistics revealed that mainland indigenous elements (including Torres Strait Islanders) featured in 95 marine incidents, Papuans featured in 48 marine incidents and South Sea Islanders featured in 149 marine incidents. The approach to colonial history at least in the Australian context, in recent times, has been to talk or hypothesise about Settler Colonial Studies. This approach to the history of New World nations such as the United States of America, Canada, Oceania and Australia is to focus on and emphasise white settler contact with indigenous elements.[172] The lexicon for this historiography includes terms such as frontiers of elimination or exploitation by settlers of indigenes or frontiers of indigenous resistance.

Therefore, adopting the term marine frontier does not appear novel or problematic. Furthermore, to keep the paradigm and say white traders dominated this particular frontier is equally

---

[172] See works of Henry Reynolds and Patrick Wolfe.

uncontroversial. After all, the Sydney mercantile class alleged, in their rejection of the Kidnapping Act of 1872 (Imp), that the trade had been in the hands of the merchants of Sydney since 1806 and it was of very great importance to the port of Sydney. It employed numerous vessels, a large amount of capital, and many of their seafaring men; and beyond all that, it gave employment to many hundreds and even thousands of natives of the South Sea Islands.[173] To take the trader class and say there was within this class a well-defined sub-group specialising in the supply of labour to Queensland would not appear to disturb the group's integrity.

The study revealed that the port of Sydney had a long history of traders operating in the South Pacific Ocean and amongst the islands of the South Pacific. Whenever a new commodity was found, the merchants of Sydney outfitted vessels to exploit the commodity. It is also clear that South Sea Islanders were on the trading vessels not only as sailing crew but as labourers to harvest, collect, process and load the items of trade.

MAINLAND INDIGENES.

On the erection of the colony of Queensland, NSW traders were the first group to exploit the abundance of bêche-de-mer within Queensland waters and are also credited with finding pearlshell in the Torres Strait. NSW traders also introduced South Sea Islanders into the pearlshell and bêche-de-mer fisheries in Queensland waters as divers and collectors of these products.

Robert Towns of NSW introduced South Sea Islanders into the Queensland workforce to meet labour shortages in the agricultural and horticultural industries of Queensland. He also

---

173 See page 69 above.

owned and operated labour vessels to transport the island labour to Queensland.

What disturbed this developing trade in Queensland was the enactment of the Kidnapping Act of 1872 by the Imperial Parliament. The perception of the Colonial Office was that a system had grown up of decoying natives onboard labour vessels, and transporting them by force to the settlement in the Fiji Islands. The Act gave power to the Royal Navy cruisers to put a stop to kidnapping. Although the Act created a statutory offence of kidnapping and did away with the uncertainty of the common law offence of kidnapping, it made simultaneously the statutory offence of carrying natives with draconian penalties. The simple act of a ship carrying black passengers in the South Pacific was prohibited unless licensed. Then the Pacific Islanders Protection Acts 1872 and 1875 (Imp) authorised British vessels to carry native labourers for any fishery, industry, or occupation in connection with the said vessel. However, the Pacific Island Labourers Act of 1884 (Qld) restricted the employment of Melanesians in Queensland to 'tropical and sub-tropical agriculture', which essentially meant the sugar industry and, in 1892, they were precluded from working in sugar mills.

Through government (Imperial and Queensland) intervention, traders were forced to give up South Sea Islanders if they wished to operate in the Queensland bêche-de-mer industry. This forced bêche-de-mer traders to source labour from mainland indigenous tribes, predominately, from the Cape York Peninsula.

In Queensland coastal and reef waters, "it was found that two types of activity emerged from the data: Bêche-de-mer fishers and Other. The category Other covered a broad range of activities. However, irrespective of the activity, when a vessel within this group, for whatever reason, found themselves shipwrecked, windbound or with shore parties on the Queensland foreshore or coastal islands, they were attacked by Aboriginals domiciled at the place of anchor or landing."[174]

In the category Other, from 1859 to 1901, there were 20 marine incidents involving Aboriginals and Torres Strait Islanders. Indigenous Australians killed 50 white men and one Aboriginal, who were shipwrecked or shore parties.[175]

In the Bêche-de-mer industry, within the relevant period, 75 marine incidents occurred in which 124 persons were killed or murdered. The predominant causes of death were attacks by myall blacks and binghi crews. A further category of death was the drownings of binghi crews.[176]

Number of Deaths by Cause

Race Killed	Myall Attacks	Binghis Attacks	Others[177]	Total Killed
European/White	9	32	1	42
Asian	5	10	nil	15
Kanakas	4	5	5	14
Binghis	1	6	46	53

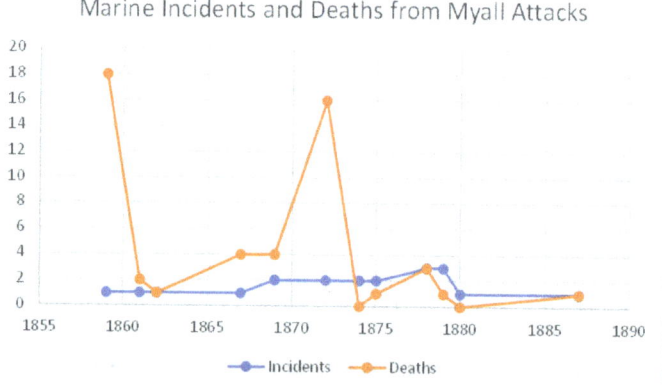

---

174 *Bêche-de-mer and the Binghis* by Paul Dillon, ISBN: 9780994638144, 2022, p 56.
175 Ibid., p 57.
176 Ibid., p 58. Myall blacks and binghi crews are Australian indigenous natives.
177 Other is a mixed-race category and it cannot be assumed that as a class they were exclusively white men and includes deaths by drowning or missing at sea.

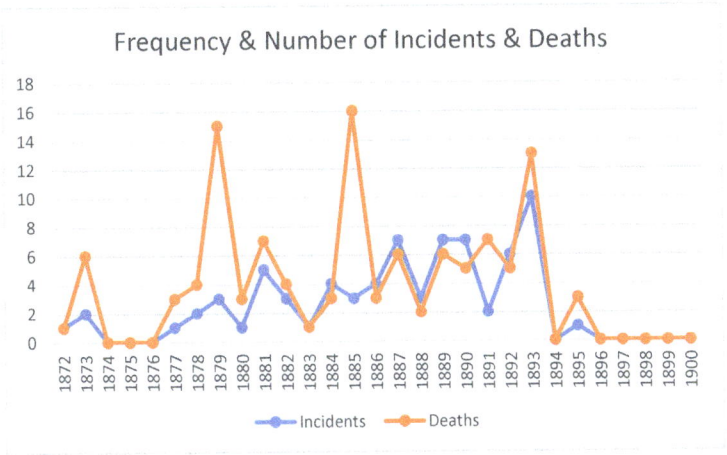

Graph 3 - Bêche-de-mer Industry (Queensland)

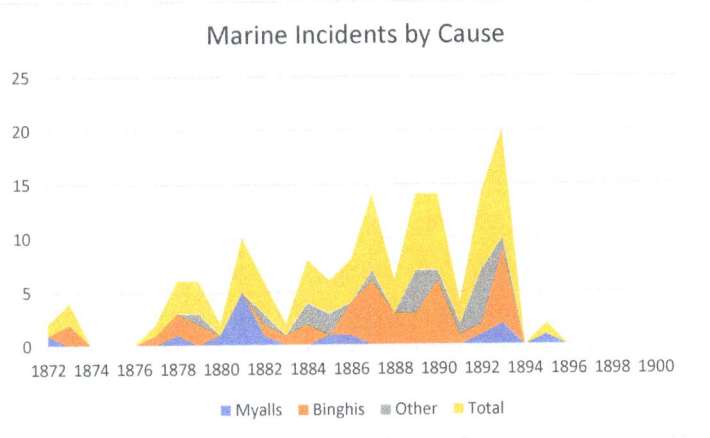

There were 95 marine incidents in Queensland waters and adjacent islands which involved mainland Aboriginals and Torres Strait Islanders. Arising out of these incidents, the number of deaths by race was as follows:

Deaths from Marine Incidents involving Aboriginal and Torres Strait Islanders

Race	Number Killed
White men	92
Aboriginal	54
Asian	15
Kanakas	14
Total	175

Graph 1 above revealed that in 1872, 14 shipwrecked white men were killed by Aboriginals. Lieutenant John Gowlland was instructed by Sir James Martin, Q.C., Attorney-General of New South Wales to take the steamer *Governor Blackall*, from Sydney to the wreck of the *Maria* and search for survivors. On 28 March 1872, Lieutenant John Gowlland informed the Attorney-General of his return to Sydney Harbour, with thirty-four survivors of the crew and passengers of the brig *Maria*, wrecked on the Bramble Reef, on 26 February 1872. The following is an abridged version of his report:

> Having received on board Sub-lieutenant Jones, from the *Basilisk*, to aid in the search, as well as a detachment of native police under the command of Mr Johnstone, for whose services I had made application to Mr Sheridan, the Police Magistrate at Cardwell - we started shortly after noon of Sunday, 17 March, to commence the examination of the coast and seaboard lying between Point Cooper and Cardwell.
>
> Every native camp between Cardwell and Point Cooper, a distance of about fifty miles, was visited and minutely searched

for any traces of white men that might permit us to hope that none of our missing countrymen might even still be alive, though languishing in captivity.

The assistance rendered to the searching parties by Mr. Johnstone and his detachment of native police was, from his accurate knowledge of the habits of the natives and his professional skill, of inestimable value to the expedition. Killed by blacks: Messrs Davis, Stratham, Parnell, Polin, O'Malley, Hardy, Williams, Dalgleish, Thompson, Heakman, Hooker, Rome, Solomon, Angel.[178]

Graph 2 above revealed that there were three periods in the study when deaths in the bêche-de-mer industry peaked, 1879, 1885 and 1893.

The Pearl-shell and Bêche-de-mer Fishery Act of 1881 provided that Polynesian (kanakas) and aboriginal natives of Australia or New Guinea, or the adjacent islands had to be employed under a written agreement recorded in the nearest Custom House or shipping office. Section 13 required all deaths and desertions of Polynesians or native labourers to be reported to the principal officer of the nearest Customs office.

The Native Labourers' Protection Act of 1884, was enacted to make better provision for preventing the improper employment of aboriginal natives of Australia or New Guinea, or of the adjacent islands on vessels trading in Queensland waters. The government of the day believed that the recruitment of Aboriginal labourers to the bêche-de-mer industry was by coercive techniques such as trickery, intimidation, or violence. Furthermore, the captain of the vessel kept no record of the abducted crew, which led to other abuses such as poor treatment of the crew, with the extreme possibility that the kidnapped crew might be abandoned without their wages and entitlements or left for dead. Therefore,

---

178 Brisbane Courier 4 April 1872 p 3.

the following penalty clauses applied:

> 6. If any vessel trading in Queensland Waters carries any native labourer with respect to whom the provisions of this Act have not been observed, the master and owner shall be jointly and severally liable to a penalty not exceeding one hundred pounds.
>
> 7. If the master or owner of any such vessel, or any other person, discharges a native labourer who has been employed on board any such vessel or pays his wages otherwise than as is herein provided, he shall be liable to a penalty not exceeding twenty pounds.
>
> 8. If any such vessel arrives in any port in Queensland having a less number of native labourers on board than are carried on the ship's articles, the master and owner shall each be liable to a penalty not exceeding five and twenty pounds for every native labourer so deficient in respect of whom such master or owner shall not prove to the satisfaction of the Court that he has been prevented by circumstances beyond his control from bringing such native labourer to such port.[179]

The 1879 surge in deaths arose in the following manner: in August, a boat had come adrift from the *Spray* with ten natives onboard. The master found the mast and sail of the boat on a sandbank but could find no trace of the missing men or the boat. The Aboriginals were missing at sea, presumed drowned. Following on from that, mainland blacks attacked the *Bowen* and the *Spray* killing three binghis, one white man and two Chinese.

From 1887, the following murders and outrages occurred in the industry:

| Chance | 16/2/1887 | Jardine River | Myalls kill Goodshaw |
| Florence | 21/2/1887 | Archer Point | Binghis steal cutter |

---

179 Supplement to the Queensland Government Gazette, 20 November 1884, No. 93, p 1737, 48 Vict. No. 20. See Hansard LC 30 September 1884 pp 109-111.

Coral Sea	June 1887	Cape Bedford	Binghis put whites overboard 1 died
Rotumah	11/10/1887	Hamilton Island	1 white crew killed by binghi over food
Lizzie	6/10/1887	Albany Island	Binghis kill Malay & attack Capt.
Fiji	18/10/1887	Barrier Reef	Binghis abandoned black Capt. & mate
Spitfire	Nov 1887	Conflict Island	Binghis kill McNair, return home
Petrel	May 1888	Cape Kimberly	Binghi kill Capt. Louis
Tam O'Shanter	August 1888	Batavia River	Binghis put Capt. Mogg overboard
Mary	Nov 1888	Batavia River	Vessel stolen by binghis
Wild Duck	March 1889	Barrier Reef	3 whites killed by kanaka & binghis
Rotumah	12/7/1889	Thursday Is.	John Williams sailed with 7 binghis
Peg	12/6/1889	Claremont Isles	Binghis steal *Peg* & desert
Mecca	3/1/1890	Sir Charles Hardy Group	Binghis killed Pratt & stole *Mecca*
Ada	April 1890	Cape Grenville	Billy Wilson beaten by binghis
Alice, lugger	May 1890	Haggerstone Is.	Burstow & Maynard attacked by binghis
Annie, lugger	May 1890	Haggerstone Is.	Charlie Weir, kanaka murdered by binghis
Ruby, cutter	31/10/1890	M Reef	Binghis kill Capt., mate & kanaka
Alert	8/12/1890	Warrior Island	Binghis steal lugger

During those years, there was a native police camp at Paterson whose duty it was to keep the natives in control. Despite this, the murders continued. The native police actions against the natives did no good. The guilty natives invariably escaped for want of evidence.

Paterson camp was disbanded at the end of 1890, and Mr. Sub-Inspector Savage took in hand the mainland natives. He paid periodic visits to their camps and enlisted the sympathy of the chiefs and tribes, whom he held responsible for the good behaviour of the tribe. The natives were known, as their descriptions were recorded on shipping records as crew. The chief was interviewed and strengthened in his position. A brass chest plate and a suit of clothes, with a few stores, had a wonderful effect on the various chiefs. The police demanded the capture of the natives who were wanted. They were captured, and the chief was called upon to give them a proper trial and, if satisfied of their guilt, to punish them. The police thus punished some of the ringleaders of the 1890 murders.

The result of this tribal system had a splendid effect on the natives, for not a single murder occurred from the time it was instituted until 1892. When the mission station was formed in 1892, the police gave up their work to the missionaries. Then the murders began again:

Curlew	January 1893	Barrier Reef, Bowen	Binghis abandoned by Capt.
Unknown	13/5/1893	Forbes Island	Binghis kill G. Waters
Leonora	27 May 1893	Seven Rivers	Binghis kill Manilla men Kintu, Pascual
Miranda	1/6/1893	Bathurst Bay	Myalls kill 2 Japanese crew
Blackfish	24/6/1893	Boydong Cay	Binghis attack 3 Manilla men, 1 died
Unknown	October 1893	Burke Island	Binghis threw H. Nicholls overboard
Alice, lugger	18/10/1893	Mapoon	Binghis kill Mobeck & Oien
Wren, lugger	November 1893	Skardon River	Binghis kill C Bruce & S Rowe
Beryl	November 1893	Night island	Myalls kill Greenlaw & Jones
Darn	26/11/1893	Batavia River	Binghis steal lugger

On 16 December 1893, John Douglas, Government Resident, Thursday Island wrote to the Colonial Secretary concerning the above bêche-de-mer outrages:

They have occurred almost invariably in boats or on stations wholly manned or carried on by native labourers. The cases I refer to are generally those in which there is a starvation allowance of food. I have, however, known cases where murder has been committed by the natives in pure revenge for personal injuries and insults. But in the majority of cases, the moving cause in the perpetration of outrages is the desire to return home. But whether they are fed well or ill, whether they are treated badly or not, there comes over them, long before the expiry of their legal agreement, an irrepressible desire to return to their own country and their tribal usages. They talk of this among themselves. Then they agree to seize the first favourable opportunity and make a dash for freedom. If they get a chance, they run away with the boat, making straight for the mainland, landing anywhere they can, and abandoning the boat. If they find they cannot do this without killing their master, they avail themselves of the first opportunity and knock him on the head or pitch him overboard.

It may be asserted; indeed, it has been broadly asserted by the local Press, which is of an exceptionally unprincipled and inexperienced type that the present outbreak of atrocities is due to the presence of the Moravian missionaries under the auspices of the Presbyterian Federal Church at the Batavia River. It is further stated that the hands of the police are tied by the fact that the missionaries have impeded their action and checked their efficiency. The statements thus made are most untrue and most preposterous. Indeed, both Mr. Sub-Inspector Savage and Senior-constable Conroy have suffered seriously in health from the hardships, they have sometimes had to undergo while camping out. It is very evident to me that it will be necessary to adopt some means to stop these outrages. In the meantime, I propose not to allow natives from the mainland to be shipped except in boats where there is a sufficient proportion of South Sea Islanders, Malays, and Japanese to render their presence harmless. John Douglas.[180]

With the introduction of the Aboriginals Protection Act on 15

---

[180] Brisbane Courier 3 January 1894 p 6 & Telegraph 3 January 1894 p 5. See also Editorial, Brisbane Courier 4 January 1894 p 4; Mackay Mercury 1 January 1894 p 3 & Mackay Mercury 11 Jan 1894 p 2.

December 1897, the appointment of W.E. Roth as Northern Protector, and his appointment as an inspector under the Pearlshell and Bêche-de-mer Fishery Act, Aboriginal labour was completely controlled. Aboriginals could no longer be employed at large; permits were required, which greatly restricted their movement and employment.

BRITISH NEW GUINEA.

Papuan natives caused 124 European deaths in 48 marine incidents. These non-Papuan deaths are identified as follows:

Deaths per each European Group[181]

Royal Navy	Missionary	Fishery	Trader	Explorer
nil	6	91	20	7

Chart 1

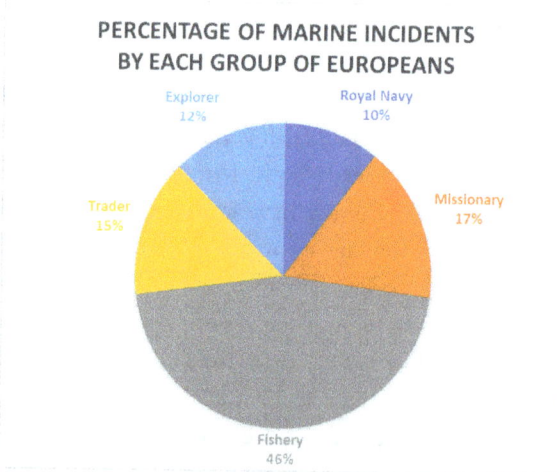

---

[181] Note European in this context may include non-whites acting as servants or agents of whites.

Chart 2 - British New Guinea[182]

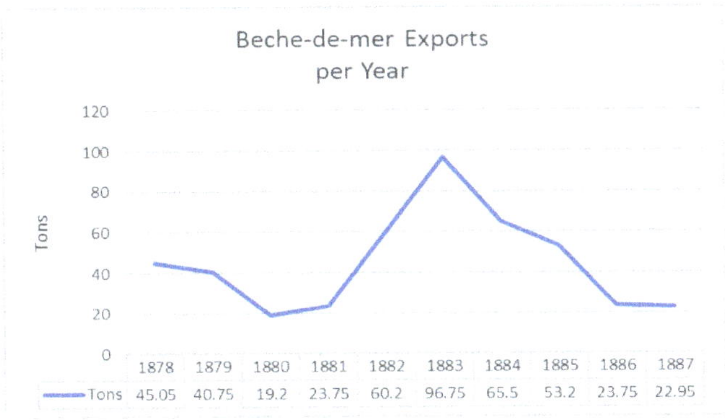

Beche-de-mer Exports
per Year
Tons
120
100
80
60
40
20
0
1878 1879 1880 1881 1882 1883 1884 1885 1886 1887
Tons 45.05 40.75 19.2 23.75 60.2 96.75 65.5 53.2 23.75 22.95

Graph 4 - British New Guinea

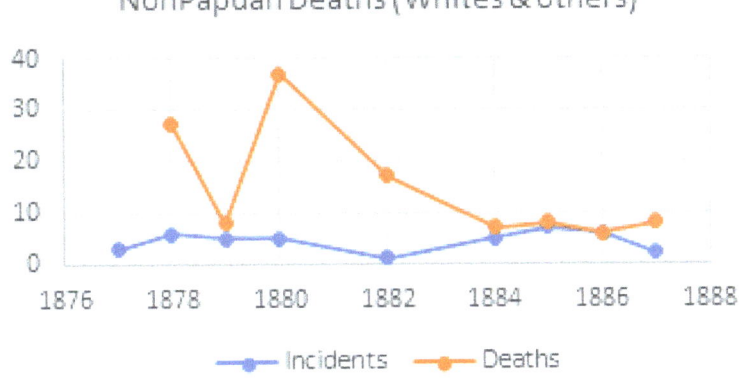

Number of Marine Incidents and
NonPapuan Deaths (Whites & others)
40
30
20
10
0
1876 1878 1880 1882 1884 1886 1888
Incidents
Deaths

The study once again revealed that bêche-de-mer fishers were the most vulnerable group of Europeans in New Guinea and adjacent island waters. The simple explanation appears to be because they had the most frequent and intimate contact with each of the indigenous groups.

The reader needs to understand that there was a significant difference in the way the fishery was conducted in New Guinea

182 British New Guinea, Report for 1888, Queensland 1889, Appendix F p 33.

waters. The fisher would visit each village and buy the dried bêche-de-mer from the indigenous native or enter into an exclusive contract with the villager to supply the fisher to the exclusion of all other fishers. Whereas in Queensland, the fisher was forced to employ Aboriginals as labourers to gather and process the fish, a far greater risk to the fisher.[183]

Graph 4 above revealed a high death rate in 1878 which peaked in 1880 with thirty deaths. Then the rate levelled off and remained at an average of 4.5 deaths per year until 1887. Chart 1 above revealed that the European group that suffered the most deaths were bêche-de-mer fishers, which accounted for 73% of the total deaths. Chart 2 revealed annual bêche-de-mer exports in tons from British New Guinea.

On 21 January 1879, the Rev. W. Lawes wrote to Sir A. Gordon, High Commissioner for the Western Pacific as follows:

> The discovery of quantities of bêche-de-mer along the coast has already led to several vessels going from Australian ports. The men on board these vessels are of the worst character, and as they have their vessels to escape in there is but little self-interest to induce them to respect native rights. It is from these vessels that difficulties have already arisen with the natives, as reported in the colonial papers. In none of these journeys or voyages, was I molested.[184]

At the Inter-colonial Conference of 1881 held in Sydney, Mr. A. Palmer, of Queensland, moved that in the opinion of this Conference, Her Majesty's attention be drawn to the outrages between the natives of many of the islands in the Pacific and British traders in those seas.[185] The Inter-colonial Conference recommended more effectual punishment of natives for any

---

183 Toil, Travel, and Discovery in British New Guinea by Bevan, Theodore Francis, 1890, London: Kegan Paul, Trench, Trübner p 147.

184 A & P C. 3617, Enclosure in No. 32, p 100.

185 Argus 29 January 1881 p 9, abridged.

crimes against British subjects and more frequent visits of Her Majesty's ships among the islands.

The Protectorate was declared on 6 November 1884 together with the appointment of Major General P. H. Scratchley, who served from 22 November 1884 to 2 December 1885, dying in office. Sir Peter Scratchley noted in his diary as follows:

> Wednesday, October 7, 1885. I am satisfied that these traders are often reckless, unscrupulous, brutal, and piratical. They cheat the natives and are apt to appeal to their revolvers. I cannot feel any sympathy for such men. They go where they have no business to. They are a thorn in my side, and I do not think the life of any white man should be risked in avenging their deaths.[186]

On 2 April 1886, Rear Admiral Tryon wrote to the Admiralty concerning the principal cases handled by officers in command of Her Majesty's ships on the northern part of the Australian station during the latter part of the season of 1885.

Tryon advised that Sir Peter Scratchley wrote to him to say how indebted he felt for the assistance rendered him by Captain Clayton, and expressed his high opinion of his judgment. He also wrote, under date 13 November 1885, on the subject of those who were sent "to collect bêche-de-mer, &c., in vessels unsuitable for the work, insufficiently manned, and worked in a manner that could end only one way, i.e., the killing, sooner or later, of the wretched masters and crews." He considered that "licences for such trade should only be given to properly manned and found vessels."

Tryon further advised that "the difficulty in dealing with outrage cases is not a little increased by the fact that tribes are very numerous in the islands, and by the absence of recognised chiefs.

---

186 Australian Defences and New Guinea compiled from papers of Peter Scratchley, by Kinloch-Cooke, Clement, London, Macmillan, 1887 p 337.

It is in the tribal or family capacity that action is taken by them, and it is this that makes it most difficult to apply a system that is in accord with modern civilisation and law, to have the same deterrent effect on Papuan races as it has on those who belong to civilised nations, and for whose benefit those laws, the outcome of centuries, exist; but a few years of patience and firmness, with moderation, will doubtless do much, and will soon stop the action of those savage races whose customs and traditions embrace the killing of a man for the sake of his head or other wanton reasons."[187]

J. Douglas, Special Commissioner for New Guinea in his 1886 report said that since the establishment of the protectorate, trade between Australia and New Guinea had died out and that the valuable pearlshell and bêche-de-mer fisheries were now abandoned on account of the numerous murders of those engaged in them, which had been permitted to go unpunished, and it was no longer safe for a white man to show his face on the coast.[188]

SOUTH PACIFIC LABOUR TRADE.

There were 149 incidents, which are tabulated and analysed under the following headings: judicial trial or administrative inquiry, Royal Navy intervention, wrecks, attacks on boat's crew, and attacks on ships. The total number of islander deaths and deaths of white men are also set out in the table below. These mortality figures include deaths arising out of shipwrecks and killings from collisions between whites and islanders.

---

[187] Papers relative to Armed Reprisals inflicted upon Natives of various Islands in the Western Pacific by H.M.S. *Diamond*. House of Commons, 25 September 1886, 51—Sess. 2, p 3. http://nla.gov.au/nla.obj-1371006542 (images 5-13, file 6815).

[188] Brisbane Courier 11 March 1887 p 3 & 23 March 1887 p 2.

MARINE INCIDENTS BY TYPE

Trial/Inquiry	RN Intervention	Wrecks	Attacks on boat crews	Attacks on ships	SSI deaths	white men deaths
55	42	34	54	5	316	58

For these marine incidents to have any meaning, the data needs to be put against the background of the overall shipping activity in the study. There were 816 outward-bound journeys with returnees for their home islands and 784 inward journeys with recruits, for the period 1868 to 1905, 1600 journeys.[189]

The data thrown up by the study of the Queensland marine frontier and its interaction with South Sea Islanders revealed or highlighted multiple areas of interest worthy of investigation and evaluation. The group, Attacks on Boat Crews and Ships, revealed that there were 54 attacks on boat crews while recruiting and 5 attacks on ships. The loss of life under these headings was for islanders 56 and whites 39. All the deaths of the whites were at the hands of islanders except for the *Ariel* where the death was by suicide and for the *May Queen* where the death was by drowning.

On 21 January 1887, G. Tryon, Commander of the Australian Station made the following observations when reporting to the Admiralty concerning the labour trade:

> 5. Natives act as a tribe or a community. They hold the white men responsible for the acts of (all) white men, and too often acts of retaliation by natives have fallen on innocent white men; it falls on the next comer who exposes himself.
>
> 6. That the natives do not value life as we do, that many are cannibals, that they kill men on certain state occasions, such as the launching of a canoe, or because of the non-return of natives that have gone to Queensland, or because no payment has been

---
[189] See page 213 below.

made on account of their non-return, has been shown; and it will not be disputed that they have many barbarous practices.

7. It can be shown that many white men trust themselves among the natives every year, notwithstanding the facts related above; and the labour traffic, the cases that occur are not many and the causes can be usually traced.

8. Admitting that the acts of natives are characterised by deceit, cruel treachery, and cold-blooded murder, these strong terms are also true of white men in too many instances, and strong as they are they are the very words used by the Royal Commission when commenting on the conduct of the government agent and master of the *Hopeful*.

9. The records of the Station show that the punishment inflicted by natives on white men at times falls on innocent white men; and when a white man falls, the officers of H.M. ships are appealed to shoot and destroy in revenge, and a section of the Press and certain writers deplore the "apathy" of H.M. naval officers, who, responsible for their every act, carefully weigh every case before they act.

11. Natives cannot be believed off-hand when one tribe throws blame on another. Such difficulty exists in obtaining the truth. The man who strikes the blow can hardly be held more guilty than those who decreed the sentence; he simply was the first in the race to give effect to it. Again, the wrong men are apt to be given up in place of the real offenders.

13. Though the natives in the New Hebrides, as a rule, have now experience in labour traffic, and can distinguish between Fijian, Queensland, and other ships. Very few cases of disorder have been reported this year in the New Hebrides.

17. I distinctly connect the massacres, as they are called, by natives, with the massacres and evildoings perpetrated by white men previously, and to the labour traffic.

18. The returned recruits used freely to take rifles and ammunition back with them. The islanders are now largely armed with rifles,

have ammunition, and are good shots. This circumstance alone renders it difficult to act punitively without sacrificing life, and the means that were formerly sufficient to punish are not sufficient at this time.

19. The natives are not wanting in intelligence: they know now how to escape when they have done wrong. In many cases, a man-of-war is powerless to act punitively.

22. The importation of labourers from the islands to Queensland ceases on 31 December 1890, under *The Queensland Pacific Island Labourers Act*, 10 November 1885, which amends the Act of 1880, and puts a limit to its operation. When this desideratum is arrived at, I consider the chief and by far the most numerous causes of bloodshed will be removed.

On 23 November 1893, after an interview with the Marquis of Ripon and Sydney Buxton, M.P., Under Secretary of State for the Colonies, Dr. Paton drew up a memorandum setting forth what he considered to be the present aspect of the Traffic—omitting all reference to the Traffic as conducted previously to 1885, when it was proved before the Supreme Court and the Royal Commission to be a system of fraud, kidnapping, and murder.[190]

On 13 January 1894, John Bramston replied:

> There appears therefore to be no sufficient reason for concluding that abuses still prevail to such an extent as to make it expedient or desirable that Her Majesty's Government should take the extreme step of suppressing all recruiting by British ships. Lord Ripon remarks that you do not mention any case drawn from your own experience and that the opinions that you offer, and those which you quote, differ materially from the recorded opinions of other authorities on the subject, such as those of the late Bishop of Melanesia, of the Bishop of Tasmania, of the Bishop of

---

190 THE KANAKA LABOUR TRAFFIC, PMB 1123 Reel 1, p 34. The reference is to the *Hopeful* case.

Brisbane, of the Convener of the Queensland Presbyterian Mission; as well as of the Governor of Queensland, from whom frequent and detailed reports are received.[191]

There were still some unsatisfactory features of the employment of these islanders in Queensland. On 11 March 1895 in the Supreme Court at Brisbane, Joseph Vos, the captain, George Thomas Olver, the Government agent, Michael Joseph Curry, the recruiter, Alfred Cuthbert Hall, chief mate, Arthur Absolam and Alfred Dowsett, seamen, of the *William Manson*, were arraigned upon a charge of kidnapping while engaged in the Pacific Island labour traffic. They pleaded not guilty. The prisoners were alleged to have carried away Erringa, Sooquow, and Zeelotta without their consent on 21 May 1894, from Malaita. After a lengthy trial, the accused were found not guilty.

The next major incident involved the *Rio Loge* at Feu, on the west side of Malaita. On landing, an incident developed between the returnees and the waiting natives over their luggage. On investigation by the Royal Navy, it was found that Bergin, the recruiter, had fired first and that the natives had in returning fire killed Bergin. As a result, the Royal Navy declined to act against the natives.

The annual reports of the Queensland Immigration department in the final decade of the labour trade reported that boat crews were fired on without any cause and crews returned fire, without casualties on either side.

SUMMATION.

The data obtained from the study of indigenous interaction with the Queensland marine frontier when tabulated revealed:

---

191 Ibid., pp 50-51.

Queensland Marine Frontier

Category	Mainland & TI Indigenes	Papuan Indigenes	Pacific Islander Indigenes
Incidents	95	48	149
White men killed	92	124	37
Indigenes killed	54	unknown	56

Perhaps the first observation to make is that whenever white men entered tribal lands or waters of uncontacted indigenes, there was a very high risk of a collision between the indigenous natives and the white party which could and often did lead to the death of those involved. The reasons for this are numerous and highly speculative.

However, on the well-established Queensland trader frontier interaction with indigenes either for raw materials or for engaging them in collecting or extracting raw materials, the study revealed that, on occasions, collisions occurred, which resulted in death, injury or property damage. Where the Government had exclusive jurisdiction over indigenes such as mainland Aboriginals and Torres Strait Islanders, native police units where tasked with investigating the collisions. The results of these investigations were, in the majority of cases inconclusive. Invariably by the time native police reached the scene of the crime, the perpetrators were long gone and or the crime scene was so degraded that little physical evidence remained. In the cases of the *Maria*, *Louisa Maria*, *Riser* and Mrs Watson, native police detachments engaged the offending Aboriginals and killed some. Even when the accused Aboriginal was taken into custody and brought before the courts, they were invariably released for want of evidence or the unavailability of an interpreter; see the case of *Spitfire*. In all other cases, native police action was ineffective. Native police camps were located at Coen, and Paterson from 1888 to 1890. They were mounted and equipped with breech-loading Snider rifles. The native police had the use of the police cutter *Eileen* from 1886 to 1890. In May 1894, to exercise greater supervision over the bêche-de-mer fisheries, the district of Thursday Island was extended to the adjacent islands and the eastern and western coasts of the Northern peninsula. Patrols would be accomplished by a steamer; the whole district being placed under the charge of Sub-Inspector Urquhart. The sub-inspector held a master mariner's certificate. Nevertheless, their use on the marine frontier was limited. In 1897, Thursday Island police station reverted to the charge of a senior sergeant consisting of 7 white police and 2 trackers.

Noel Loos in *Invasion and Resistance Aboriginal-European relations on the North Queensland frontier 1861-1897*, divided his study into four frontiers. The relevant frontier is the sea frontier. Loos identified 119 settlers and their employees killed as a result of Aboriginal resistance in North Queensland between 1861 and 1897.[192] His final comment on the matter is:

> Finally, the appendix does not even attempt to list the Aborigines killed in resisting the invasion by Europeans, Chinese settlers and their employees of other races. To suggest that at least ten times as many Aborigines were killed for every intruder killed seems very conservative when one considers that Aborigines were often killed to drive them from runs and river valleys and for merely disturbing or killing cattle and horses, let alone killing or wounding settlers. One also has to remember that Native Police detachments were constantly involved in punitive raids and dispersals from 1861 to 1896 in North Queensland and that the settlers were unrestrained in their use of force throughout this period. Thus, to suggest that at

---

192 Invasion and Resistance Aboriginal-European relations on the North Queensland frontier 1861-1897, Noel Loos, ANU Press, Canberra, 1982, p 193. Loos noted: This table then cannot claim to be an accurate assessment of the loss of life resulting from Aboriginal resistance. Author: Neither do I claim to have made a definitive assessment of the loss of life from indigenous predation.

least 4,000 Aborigines died as a result of frontier resistance in North Queensland between 1861 and 1896 is probably so conservative as to be misleading.[193]

The reader needs to appreciate that Loos' assertion that the deaths of Aboriginals by white settlers and traders on each of his four frontiers were a result of Aboriginal insurgency or military resistance against whites is nothing more than speculation. The word "resistance" as used by Loos is in the sense of organised opposition to an invader.[194] The proposition is absurd for the following reasons first, the empirical data does not support the contention that Aboriginals conducted themselves as an organised resistance movement, and second, by definition, Aboriginal clans were dis-organised, lacked a lingua franca and did not collaborate with each other nor were there within the clans a hierarchical structure of leadership and leader fealty.

The Black Armband Brigade of which Loos is a leading member maintains that the predominant and principal source of Aboriginal deaths on the colonial frontier was by white settlers or their agents, in particular, the native police. This school of thought commenced with H Reynolds postulating that 20,000 Aboriginals were killed by frontier conflict. Reynolds offered no proof, but simply asserted that the proposition was self-evident.

Given that an aspect of this study is a comparison across the board of each of the indigenous groups, epidemiology arises as well as the use of lethal force. In each indigenous group, the Black Armband Brigade have postulated that the predominant and principal cause of death of the indigenous group was settler violence and poor living conditions coupled with harsh treatment

---

193 Ibid., p 190.

194 The History Wars is a tiresome subject much driven by leftwing historians pursuing a political agenda of destroying the colonial history of white Australia while advancing the political aspirations of an Austral métis (Anglo-Aboriginal) alleging indigenous bloodlines.

of the native inhabitants. In the case of South Sea Islanders, Ralph Shlomowitz addressed the issue in *Epidemiology and the Pacific Labor Trade*.[195]

Queensland Period	Average Number of Deaths per annum	Average Population at Risk	Average Annual Death Rate per 1,000
1879-1887	735	8,916	82
1888-1892	471	8,812	53
1893-1906	285	8,239	35

Based on the above table, Shlomowitz observed:

> The long-term decline in death rates is striking: from 82 per 1,000 (1879-1887) to about 60 per 1,000 (1882-1892), to about 35 per 1,000 (1893-1910s). The long-term decline in mortality was (from a) built-up of immunities to these illnesses.[196]

> The hypothesis that the high death rates were the result of poor living conditions and harsh treatment does not explain the empirical findings listed above.[197]

> Since there is no substantial evidence that the mortality rates of Pacific Island migrants were linked to their living and working conditions, it follows that, even if the migrants had been treated much more humanely, their death rates would still have been high. They would still have been exposed to a new disease environment, and their congregation on ships, in depots waiting transshipment, and on plantations would have increased the spread of contagious illnesses.[198]

The Royal Navy, Australian Station, adopted a policy of lethal force in the South Seas. With their four men-of-war and five armed schooners, the Royal Navy had more than an adequate platform from which to engage blackbirding vessels and

---

195 The Journal of Interdisciplinary History, Spring, 1989, Vol. 19, No. 4 (Spring, 1989), pp. 585-610.
196 Ibid., p 598.
197 Ibid., p 599.
198 Ibid., p 600.

predatory islanders. On occasion, the Navy shelled villages and landed armed parties of marines and sailors, who were not only instructed to capture suspects but to carry out acts of war against villagers by burning their dwellings, destroying their canoes, chopping down coconut trees and other fruit trees as well as destroying gardens. The following is an excellent example of the Royal Navy in action:

> *H.M.S. Rosario,*
>
> At sea, Lat. 11° 32' S., Long. 169° 25' E.
>
> 25 November 1871.
>
> 2. I steamed close along the Island of Nguna, and seeing a party of natives assembled near to one of the villages which we had destroyed on the previous day, I threw a few shot and shell amongst them for the purpose of dispersing them, as I had been led to believe that the natives here were inclined to ridicule the power of a man-of-war, having been repeatedly threatened by the presence of one, without having actually come into contact with one.[199]

Although the Navy caused a good deal of property damage to island villages, the record suggested that when armed naval parties engaged natives, deaths and causality figures were low. In other words, when we compare the high-tech, state-of-the-art naval force, who killed very few natives in lethal force confrontations, to the native police, who never numbered more than about eight armed troopers in any single skirmish and caused 20,000 Aboriginal deaths, then surely this figure of 20,000 Aboriginal deaths must look doubtful, even far-fetched.

---

199 http://nla.gov.au/nla.obj-1481606654 (image 80, file 6251).

4

Review of Past Historical Treatment of the South Sea Islanders in Colonial Queensland

It is a fundamental truth that all living creatures need a habitat from which to draw sustenance. For the vast majority of living creatures, their sustenance is obtained either by gathering or hunting food suitable to their diet or taste. Human society also followed such a regime of hunting and gathering. However, in the timeline of human evolution, man lived either a nomadic or a sedentary lifestyle. In nomadic societies, human activity was limited, within the extended family or clan, to gathering or hunting for a daily sustainable diet, a hand-to-mouth economy. Where a society progressed to exploiting their habitat to produce food by either agriculture or animal husbandry, an element of organisation then entered the structure of the clan or tribe. This led to individuals being drafted off to undertake a specific task, directed to producing a specific product for which the individual was rewarded by a share of the product which he then bargained with to support himself in the necessities of life. Eventually, labour, a man's time and effort, came to be seen as a commodity.

On occasions, the man and the commodity became confused. Some societies viewed men as a commodity when, of course, the correct view is that labour is the commodity.

A further element of confusion also existed in the supply side of the labour market. Apart from human behaviour being divided into nomadic or sedentary lifestyles, the labour market was further differentiated by the existence of black or coloured people.[200] Those who identified the commodity of labour as men believed their view was reinforced by the existence of black and coloured men. If God had put the beasts of burden on earth to help man, then black men, who were everywhere in a state of savagery akin to the beasts, must also have been put on earth to work at the behest of the white man. The concept of men as a commodity of commerce is known as slavery. Although this view of labour was held for many thousands of years, a school of thought began to develop in England that slavery was immoral and unchristian. As this view developed traction in the community and ultimately in the UK parliament, and the need for labour became acute with the transition to industrial forms of production, the concept of labour became clearer in the minds of those capitalists venturing into the emerging world of mechanised production. As productivity increased through more efficient means of production, demand for raw materials multiplied. This trend was intensified by the American Civil War. Given that the economy of New South Wales, and later the colony of Queensland, were limited in their ability to exploit this huge demand for raw materials in the United Kingdom through industrialisation and supply disruption of the American market, Queensland could only offer the prospects of entering the cotton and sugar supply chain. Venture capital was made available by banks and other financiers of the day to entrepreneurs and the

---

200 There is, of course, another empirical divide in the labour market that between male and female work which is not relevant here.

Queensland government adopted policies in support of these commodities as well as passing relevant legislation enabling land and infrastructure to be acquired by the entrepreneurs.

However, the age-old issue of a sustainable supply of labour became acute in the eyes of venture capitalists. The leading investor in growing cotton, Robert Towns clearly stated the issue in his letter of 31 August 1863: he needed a cheap, reliable source of labour for his cotton plantation, and that was a regular supply of South Sea Islanders.[201] According to the testimony of Mr. Towns, South Sea Islanders met all the criteria for working on his plantation.

Thus, in Fiji and Queensland, a trade in labour sprang up, which it was said degenerated into a trade in labourers. Skippers went about picking up men, not to employ them, but to sell them at so much a head to plantation owners. In this nefarious business, there was not only gross deception and cruelty practised, but when resistance was offered there was murder. Repeated outrages were reported and the climax of iniquity was reached with the *Carl*.[202] The British Government, true to its policy of discouraging slavery, passed the Kidnapping Act of 1872 and began policing the South Seas with great vigour. The result of the Imperial legislation was satisfactory, but in another aspect, it was unsatisfactory, for it almost ruined a legitimate trade, or at least driven it away from the port of Sydney. Since the Kidnapping Act was passed, not a single slave ship was found. But the Royal Navy made up for it by snapping up several vessels engaged, not in picking up men, but in picking up shells; and the owners of these vessels, though innocent of slavery, had to pay a serve

---

[201] See pp 27-30 above.

[202] The *Carl* was not a Queensland labour vessel. The crew were tried in New South Wales and Victoria. Armstrong and Dowden were sentenced to be hanged, which was commuted to life. In May 1869, Albert Hovell, master of the *Young Australian*, and Rangi were sentenced to death in Sydney for the murder of three Paamans.

penalty. This was the unintended consequence of the Act. The owners of the *Melanie* tried to get a licence from the Governor at Sydney to employ islanders in the fishery industry. The licence was refused on the ground that the men were not 'labourers' within the meaning of the Act but were practically part of the ship's company. When the vessel was seized, the Supreme Court held that the seizure was legal because the islanders could not be held to be part of the crew, but were 'labourers' within the meaning of the Act. The Court interpreted the Act strictly and pronounced condemnation.

However, South Sea Islanders were black and *indigènes non-civilisés*. These characteristics offended sensitivities within the Queensland community of the time. And for those sections of the community who objected to the introduction of this class of workers, the major objection was that they were slaves by the self-evident fact that they were black savages. Therefore, it was immoral to allow such workers into the colony. As each new Queensland government permitted the entry of South Sea Islanders to work on sugar plantations, the debate never resolved itself. The Exeter Hall followers together with the missionaries and other sundry do-gooders continued to allege the islanders were slaves while the sugar producers and employers of the islanders maintained that the islanders were free agents and that white labour was either organically unsuited to hard labour in the tropics or demanded too high a wage thus endangering the economic viability of the sugar industry.

It is worth noting the observations of Sir A Stephen, Chief Justice to the Governor, Earl Belmore on 10 July 1869 re *Daphne*:

> That all our Imperial legislation hitherto has been directed to the case of persons carried away as slaves, or for the purpose of being dealt with as slaves. They (kanakas) may scarcely have understood the contract which the ship owners

assert they entered into or they may have been cajoled or induced by falsehoods or even threats to signify assent. But if the term of service was limited (as in Queensland it must be by law) I believe then and especially if in addition wages were fixed and a return voyage guaranteed, how can the men be legally deemed slaves?[203]

The maritime traffic between the colony of New South Wales and the South Sea Islands might be described in the following terms:

> From a maritime systems perspective, the early phase of European voyaging in Oceania can arguably be characterised as "contact" rather than "colonialism" for several reasons. Among these were the short duration of visits to many islands, a focus on ship-based interaction, the small number of permanent foreigners present on islands, and the absence of viable migrant communities. Power relations were also relatively balanced because there was no network of ports and settlements in the Pacific to support colony establishment until the nineteenth century. This is not to imply that "contact" was static and one-sided, or that early meetings did not influence colonialism.[204]

The traffic was mercantile-based, devoted entirely to trade in the commodities available from the South Sea Islands. It was a trader frontier. However, in Queensland, the trade became specialised and limited to one commodity only where the function of the trader was to recruit labour and then to transport the engaged workers to their respective ports of disembarkation. In modern times, this would be a matter viewed from the perspective of industrial relations and be dealt with under a guestworker programme. The Queensland government did legislate a

---

203 http://nla.gov.au/nla.obj-1476027682 (images 32-37, file 6162)
204 Violence in Early Maritime Encounters in the Pacific p 211, Beaule, Christine D., editor. Frontiers of Colonialism. University Press of Florida, 2017. JSTOR, https://doi.org/10.2307/j.ctvx06wxq. Accessed 15 Aug. 2023.

statutory framework under which South Sea Islanders could be employed in the colony of Queensland.

Turning now to the academic literature on the subject, apart from the scholarly works, the source material is also extensive. There is the material generated by the UK and colonial press, the Imperial government, the Admiralty and the UK parliamentary papers, together with the colonial papers located in State archives and State parliamentary papers. There are, indeed, many rabbit holes down which the supererogant researcher might spend a lifetime searching.

Clive Moore's writing in 1992 dealt with the then scholarly works available on the historiography of immigrant Melanesians in Australia.[205] He wrote as follows:

> A change in interpretation is evident in the 1960s and 1970s when Canberra based historians such as Dorothy Shineberg (1967), Deryck Scarr (1967; Giles 1968), and Peter Corris (1973) argued that the mobilization of labour in Melanesia last century was characterised not so much by violence and illegality as by a substantial degree of active cooperation by Islanders, who had considerable control over their lives and labour in the sandalwood trade and on sugar and coconut plantations. More recent academic studies of the Queensland labour trade have modified and extended, though not changed, the essence of this conclusion. Non-academic writers such as Holthouse (1969, 1988) continued to produce popular histories, oblivious of any revision in thought, and the media largely ignored the revision. Kay Saunders has produced the most thorough documentary study of the Queensland labour trade and made a significant theoretical contribution through her analysis of indenture and race relations. But her study grew out of an interest in colonial Queensland and the plantation as an institution. In seeming contradiction to Scarr and Corris, she argued for greater

---

205 Revising the Revisionists: The Historiography of Immigrant Melanesians in Australia, Clive Moore, Pacific Studies, Vol. 15, No. 2--June 1992.

recognition of the exploitation and oppression of the labourers.[206]

Moore noted further:

> In Australian history early in the 1970s there was still an emphasis on the destructive impact of European capitalism and racism, typified by Saunders's major studies (1974, 1982) and Evans, Saunders, and Cronin's study focused on race relations between Europeans, Aborigines, Melanesians, and Chinese in colonial Queensland (1975). A few years later, the writings of Henry Reynolds and Noel Loos (Reynolds and Loos 1976; Loos 1982), and particularly Reynolds's *The Other Side of the Frontier* (1981), were lauded as original and path-breaking in the emphasis they gave to Aboriginal resistance. But as Kerry Howe pointed out in his review of *The Other Side of the Frontier*: "Historians of culture contact in Africa, the Americas, New Zealand and the Pacific Islands have been looking at 'the other side' for twenty to thirty years now, and many of the issues Reynolds examines are deja vu in any context other than Australian history" (1983:82; see also Howe 1988:602). Reynolds and Loos's emphasis on resistance served a useful purpose in quantifying conflict and showing that Aborigines were not passive victims, but their enthusiasm to prove the point led them to neglect Aboriginal accommodation, which was just as important to Aboriginal survival. ... are sometimes purposefully (Reynolds 1981:1), but often unwittingly, related to the needs of black radicalism at that time (Reece 1987:117). The same is true of Saunders's thesis (1974), and Evans, Saunders, and Cronin's (1975) and Ryan's (1981) books. In their preface to the 1988 edition of Race Relations in Queensland, Evans and Saunders provide an excellent description of the political milieu in which they researched and wrote and discuss their motivations.[207]

---

206 Ibid., p 62, abridged.
207 Ibid., p 72.

In a footnote to this article, Moore observed:

> 5. Perhaps the only point of disjunction remaining is that Aborigines, Melanesians (indigenous and immigrant), Chinese, and other Asian groups in Australia are usually treated as discrete entities, relating to Europeans but seldom to each other. I am indebted to Doug Munro for drawing my attention to this point.[208]

This observation allows me to remind the reader of the purpose of my three books, which is to identify not only all the marine incidents in Queensland's colonial shipping and maritime history involving indigenous elements but to compare and contrast the governance and treatment of each of the indigenous groups identified in the study: Australian Aboriginals, Torres Strait Islanders, Papuans and Pacific Islanders. Therefore, I won't be covering the field when it comes to relating the history of immigrant Melanesians in Australia. Much of the academic material identified by Moore is not relevant, in my view, to the aims and objects of this book.

In the Journal of Pacific History, 1967, Deryck Scarr published an article entitled *Recruits and Recruiters: A Portrait of the Pacific Islands Labour Trade*. It appears from the article that Mr. Scarr approached the subject of the South Sea Islander labour traffic as a single field of study when in fact the trafficking in island labour was carried on by several parties such as Queensland, Fiji, and the French government for their interests in Tahiti and New Caledonia. Such a broad bush approach may serve the purpose of providing a topical narrative of some of the highlights of the labour trade, but without clarity and precision in the identification of incidents, drawing generalised conclusions from the material seems risky and fraught with peril.

---

208 Ibid., p 78.

Scarr made the following observation:

> The exact relationship which existed between master and government agent depended on the relative strength of character of the two men involved. But in most ships, the government agent was more likely to be the victim of such indignities and some agents went in fear of their lives. After John Slade was drowned at Aneityum in 1876, it was rumoured that the boat had been deliberately upset, and the *Ethel's* government agent had a narrow escape in 1884 when the master's rifle, exploding 'accidentally', buried a bullet in the deck close to him.[209]

The above paragraph opens with a cliche that is supported by authorities that lack probative value. John Slade drowned while recruiting off Fatuna Island. The fact that an anonymous letter written to the *Brisbane Courier* eight years after the event alleged Slade was murdered by the recruiter is an absurdity, and its value as a historical source is zero. The question is, why would Scarr bother to mention the letter? His next authority is an incident on the labour vessel, *Ethel*. The government agent in this case was Mr. C Mills. There was a serious incident aboard the *Ethel*, but it wasn't the accidental discharge of a firearm. Mills, the government agent and Captain Loutit were charged with kidnapping, yet Scarr failed to mention this fact and the consequences of the kidnapping trials. This article did not advance my research topics.

The next work of interest is that of Peter Corris, *Passage, Port and Plantation A History of Solomon Islands Labour Migration, 1870-1914*, a thesis completed whilst he was a research scholar of the Department of Pacific History at the Australian National University, between January 1967 and January 1970. Incidentally, Deryck Scarr was Corris's supervisor. Again, I would describe

---

209 Recruits and Recruiters: A Portrait of the Pacific Islands Labour Trade Author(s): Deryck Scarr Source: The Journal of Pacific History, 1967, Vol. 2 (1967), p 12.

this as a whole of field study but limited to the Solomon Islands.

In chapter II, Recruiting for the Colonies, 1870-1911, Corris veered off at a tangent into slave raiding and headhunting operations conducted by the people of New Georgia, Vella Lavella, Kolombangata and Simbo. However, what is of greater importance is his statement that:

> In 1880, there were three such attacks. The Queensland schooner *Emprenza* was taken at Kolombangara in June; all members of the crew were killed, and the ship was looted and burnt. In September, the *Borealis*, a brigantine in the Queensland trade, was attacked near Uru on the west coast of Malaita. In October the Fiji schooner *Zephyr* was assailed at Choiseul. Each of these attacks appeared to be motivated by a desire for plunder and this probably also inspired the strike against the *Janet Stewart* at Kwai, Malaita, in February 1882. The islanders planned and executed the assaults upon the *Borealis* and *Janet Stewart* with great skill, sending parties of men out to the ships, ostensibly to offer themselves as recruits; once aboard they took out concealed weapons and cut down the crew and recruits who had joined the ship at other places.[210]

Unfortunately, Corris has got his facts wrong. It was not the schooner *Emprenza* but the *Esperanza*. Moreover, the *Esperanza* was not a Queensland vessel, but a schooner that hailed from Sydney; she was a trader, not a labour vessel. Furthermore, the *Borealis* was not a Queensland vessel. She was out of Auckland and in the Fiji trade. This confusion by Corris demonstrates my point that covering the field, unless one is scrupulously precise and accurate, distorts what was happening on the ground at the time. In the relevant timeframe, 1868 to 1905, Queensland only operated labour vessels, not trader vessels.

---

210 Passage, Port and Plantation A History of Solomon Islands Labour Migration, 1870-1914, Peter Corris, Thesis, ANU, 1970, p 65.

In June 1981, Clive Moore submitted a thesis entitled *Kanaka Maratta: A History of Melanesian Mackay*, a study of the migration of Malaitan (Solomon Islands) labourers between 1871 and 1904.[211] At the beginning of his thesis, Moore defined the entire Melanesian labour trade as the recruiting trade: involving some kidnapping as well as voluntary enlistment; Melanesians either enlisted voluntarily or were kidnapped or stolen.[212] He also introduced the term "Cultural Kidnapping;" those who were not physically kidnapped were certainly "culturally kidnapped". In the introduction to his thesis Moore said, "(he) examines instances of Malaitan resistance to the recruiters."[213] Then in chapter 2, Moore said, "indeed on Malaita it was essential, given the ferocity with which Malaitans resisted the advances of recruiters if they felt any grievance towards Europeans. Footnote: 58. Refer to Appendix Two: Malaitan Resistance against Europeans."[214] He then goes onto say, "The result of this resistance was often a visit from a British naval vessel, seeking out offenders and shelling their villages."[215] Finally, Moore says, "Appendix Two cataloguing examples of Malaitan resistance to recruiters must be viewed in the light of the foregoing explanation of the place of vengeance in the overall network of exchange. At the most conservative estimate possible, between seventy and one hundred Malaitans died on the island or on their way to Queensland or to some other colony as a result of resistance on their part or from European retaliation."[216]

---

211 http://eprints.jcu.edu.au/24019 The thesis is based two visits to the Solomon Islands (five months field work); a considerable amount of oral testimony; and a computer programme to resort Islander baptism, marriage and deaths.
212 Ibid., p xii.
213 Ibid., p xviii.
214 Ibid., p 88.
215 Ibid., p 125.
216 Ibid., p 142.

It is not clear to me in what sense Moore used the word 'resistance'. Table Three: Malaitan Resistance was drawn up from Appendix Two.[217] Moore recorded 30 Malaitan deaths against Queensland, with 18 white men killed by Malaitans.[218]

Kay Saunders in 1982 published *Workers in Bondage The Origins and Bases of Unfree Labour in Queensland 1824-1916*. A novice or an unlettered quirest might ask why was it necessary to import native labour into Queensland when there already was a large indigenous population of natives available. Saunders offered the following, "Settler societies, particularly those containing plantation economies like Queensland, soon found that the conquered indigenous people could not provide either the large numbers or the consistency of application to work for the new proprietors."[219]

Then Saunders makes this bold assertion:

> Clearly, the dispossessed Aborigines contributed indispensable labour services for rural graziers. For these masters, they possessed several invaluable characteristics. First, the blacks were forced to work simply for sustenance for themselves and for those other Aborigines unable to labour by reason of age or infirmity. They were accorded a meagre, nutritionally deficient diet of damper, offal, tea and sugar, and usually alcohol and sometimes later, opium. The Aborigines, as a vanquished dispossessed people, were therefore a vital ancillary to the establishment of the pastoral mode of production. Their labour

---

217 Ibid., p 123.

218 There is a difference between Moore's numbers and mine. The difference is small and in the scheme of things even if Moore's are preferred, the impact is not significantly higher. Part of the difference lies in Moore relying on oral history. He detected a bias in the oral testimony of kidnapping. One would not be surprised by a bias of killings by whites.

219 Workers in Bondage The Origins and Bases of Unfree Labour in Queensland 1824-1916 Kay Saunders, University of Queensland Press St Lucia, 1982 p xvii.

was enforced compulsory toil, without any of the safeguards, however ineffectual, of the contract worker or wage labourer. Unlike the assigned convict who also worked without wages, the blacks were not being punished for designated crimes. They could not anticipate any remission of their "sentence". They were de facto chattels bound securely to the new owners of their land. The ramifications were twofold. Firstly, their position resembled that of slaves in the Caribbean or the Ante-Bellum South, but without the protection which investment in human property conferred. In structural terms, these early Queensland sheep or cattle stations possessed a quasi-slave mode of production with the added complications of indentured and wage labour patterns. Secondly, it meant that Aborigines were permanently forced to perform all the arduous menial toil with no chance of upward socio-economic mobility. In a society where class mobility was extremely limited, Aborigines by virtue of their colour were precluded from entering this structure; they were relegated within a totally closed caste. The racial ideology of the time both rationalized and maintained these patterns.[220]

This statement is not supported by any meaningful source material. Where is the evidence that the indigenous occupants were proletarised? How does Saunders account for the employment of kanakas on sheep and cattle stations until it was banned in 1884?[221] The Master and Servant Act did not apply to the Aboriginals. There was no control and regulation of Aboriginals until the Native Labourers' Protection Act of 1884, and the Aboriginals Protection and Restriction of the Sale of Opium Act, 1897. Furthermore, any civilian restraining or imprisoning Aboriginals would be prosecuted by the police. Saunders' source, A C Grant is ambiguous in his description

---

220 Ibid., pp 12-13.

221 Pacific Island Labour Migrants in Queensland, Peter Corris, The Journal of Pacific History, 1970, Vol. 5 (1970), p 45.

of Aboriginal assistance to station management, which was nothing more than ad hoc help dependent on the availability and willingness of the Aboriginals to cooperate:

> Half a dozen young, active men and boys, in tattered breeches and boots, might always be seen hanging round the stockyards and bachelors' quarters, while a circle of happy, merry, white-toothed young women and girls would seat themselves at the back of the kitchen, and in return for little services rendered they received food, which to them were luxuries. They were of the greatest use as stockmen, trackers and shepherds, bark getters, sheep washers, followers on horseback, horse boys, and washerwomen, and, in a hundred ways, they made life in those solitudes more endurable. They went messages on foot, and on horseback. They saved labour and performed work which was outside the province of white men.[222]

Dr. W. E. Roth, Northern Protector of Aboriginals, was called to the bar of the Legislative Council, on 8 October 1901 and examined on the Aboriginals Protection and Restriction of the Sale of Opium Bill:

> By Hon. A. Gibson: Do you find Aboriginals take kindly to agricultural pursuits?
>
> Walter E. Roth: No; that is the whole secret of it. The aboriginal is a nomad, and he reasons thus to himself: If by roaming for an hour in a day I can get my food for the next twenty-four hours, why should I work seven, eight, or nine hours for a white man?
>
> Q: Just now there is a difficulty in reference to coloured labour in the cane fields. You say there are in your district 18,000 of those people, more or less. Do you think it would not be possible for the sugar planters of Queensland to employ them with advantage on the cane fields for six or eight months of the year?

---

222 A. C. Grant, "Early Station Life in Queensland", Mitchell Library, NSW pp 23, 25-26.

> Roth: The question is whether the blacks would be willing to do it. I have no right to force the blacks to work, although they are quite capable of doing it.
>
> Q: Would money not induce them to take up employment of that description?
>
> Roth: I do not think so. The blackboy notices that by working for an hour he can get food for the day, and he will not go to work for a whole day, except under compulsion. That is the difficulty; they are a nomadic people, not a settled agricultural one.
>
> Q: You do not find the aborigines on the Johnstone River going in for working on the cane fields?
>
> Roth: As a rule, the blacks will not go in for labour of that kind.[223]

The Aboriginal made and used tools with his own hands within his habitat for his use. As Roth rightly pointed out above, Aboriginals were nomads not of the proletariat: not industrial wage earners who, possessing neither capital nor production means, earned their living by selling their labour.

Saunders goes on to say:

> The Colonial Attorney-General, John Bramston, argued that the case did not constitute kidnapping in its legal sense as it was not possible to kidnap a person of a savage race if he was brought within the protection of the law … for the moment these Islanders touched the deck of an English vessel they were free and had a right of habeas corpus. (10)
>
>> 10. Regina vs. Coath. Supreme Court of Queensland, 18 December 1871. GOV/A.4 and CRS 147; Attorney-General to Governor, 22 December 1871, QSA GOV/A.4. In 1873, Bramston asked that Coath be released as Meiklejohn, the main witness for the prosecution, had

---

223 Hansard LC 8 October 1901 p 1138.

> been insane during the duration of the voyage. Bramstone (sic) to Governor, 24 September 1873.[224]

This quote from Saunders on the Coath case demonstrates that she did not understand the legal proceedings. Coath had been convicted of abducting and kidnapping nine South Sea Islanders and sentenced to 5 years' imprisonment. Coath appealed his conviction. Mr. Lilley, Q.C., and Mr. Blake, Q.C., were for the appellant prisoner, and Bramston, Attorney-General was in support of the conviction. Mr Lilley argued in support of the appeal, saying:

> The question substantially is, "What is the offence of kidnapping, as known to the English law?" Can it be committed on a savage or barbarous people captured and brought within the protection of British law, and landed free at Maryborough? The moment these islanders touched the deck of an English vessel, they were free, and had a right to habeas corpus, and they were landed at Maryborough and were allowed to land free;

In the case of McMurdo and Davies of the schooner *Stanley*, Saunders says:

> A crew member, Joseph Davies, was charged in February 1884 with kidnapping but was found "not guilty". McMurdo was discreetly tried in Suva, receiving a minimal sentence.[225]

On 3 April 1884, at the City Police Court, Brisbane, McMurdo and Capt. Davies were charged with kidnapping two islanders. Brisbane, 18 June 1884, the charge of kidnapping against Davies and McMurdo was formally withdrawn. The accused were conveyed onboard *H.M.S. Raven* to Fiji, where they were tried at the High Commissioner's Court for an alleged outrage on the Laughlan Islands and sentenced to three months imprisonment.

---

224 Saunders, 1982, p 21.
225 Saunders, 1982, p 24.

Saunders's view of the 1872 Imperial Kidnapping Act demonstrates a total lack of understanding of the legislation:

> In 1872, after the murder of Bishop John Patterson, (sic) the British Parliament passed the Kidnapping Act which provided for a £500 bond on every vessel, to be forfeited on conviction of a felony. This hardly provided a deterrent in view of the enormous profits (in excess of £2, 000) to be made on one voyage alone.[226]

The scheme of the 1872 Imperial Kidnapping Act provided for

> 3. It shall not be lawful for any British vessel to carry native labourers of the said islands, not being part of the crew of such vessel, unless the master shall have entered into a bond in the sum of five hundred pounds nor unless he shall have received a licence. The penalties under the act were a fine not to exceed £500, s 7; the maximum term of imprisonment-life, s 9; and s 18 the condemnation of the vessel and cargo and forfeiture to the Crown of the said vessel and cargo.

On the whole, Saunders's above work of 1982 did not advance the aims and objectives of this study. The final work is that of Tracey Banivanua-Mar, *Consolidating violence and colonial rule: discipline and protection in colonial Queensland.*[227]

This article reads like a catechism by the leading members of the Black Armband Brigade of the Australian School of Colonial Settler Studies. Moreover, on occasion, Banivanua-Mar misused technical terms such as:

> Queensland had received the status of a self-governing colony in 1859.[228]

> Coath served three years of his resulting five-year sentence

---

226 Saunders, 1982, p 28.
227 Postcolonial Studies, 2005, Vol. 8, No. 3, pp. 303–319.
228 Ibid., p 303.

and was released and acquitted in 1874.²²⁹

The colony of Queensland did not exist before 1859. The settlement at Brisbane was known as the Moreton Bay district. On 6 June 1859, Queen Victoria signed Letters Patent, erecting the self-governing colony of Queensland. Furthermore, John Coath was not acquitted in 1874, he was pardoned by the Governor of Queensland on 1 October 1873.²³⁰

Here are some quotes from Banivanua-Mar:

> ...the frontiers of the western Pacific labour trade, which supplied indentured labour for Queensland's sugar industry, was yet to be regulated by Imperial legislation. Queensland was thus in a loose state of transition in the 1870s as it moved from the 'killing times' of frontier colonialism to the period of regulated and bureaucratic colonisation on the inside of the frontiers.

> It builds upon an existing and foundational body of scholarship that has explored the underpinning violence of race relations in Queensland and the western Pacific at length.

> Violence it is argued did not just accompany colonial practices and imperatives by virtue of some historical accident. Rather it was structurally implied in the very activities of contact and negotiation that established colonial occupation and hegemony in Queensland.

> The violence that occurred between recruiters and Islanders on the western Pacific's frontiers was also conceptually separated from the civilised colonial project by being boxed off as the product of the chaos and lack of rationality of either times long ago, or the savageness of areas beyond the reach of civilisation's folds. Represented violence in the Pacific also bordered on the atmospheric, and massacres, kidnappings and cycles of violent retribution between Islanders and recruiters were constantly talked about.

---

229 Ibid., p 306.
230 Queensland State Archives, Item ID ITM2926845.

> Coath's case highlights the central theme of this article. Violence, and in this case frontier violence, was not a series of events that we can locate beyond the official dimensions of the colonial project. Instead, its sanction came from its carefully-crafted exteriority. Britain's Kidnapping Act of 1872 for example gave the Queensland Supreme Court jurisdiction over British subjects in any area of the Pacific not under the jurisdiction of a civilised (European) power. At the same time, however, it legalised an unquestioned jurisdiction to trade the labour of people of any unclaimed Island. Similarly, while Queensland would exert further control and surveillance over labour recruiters, these regulated conditions would also standardise the use on recruiting vessels of chains, gags, guns, handcuffs, leg irons, and straitjackets.[231]

The difficulty with Banivanua-Mar's analysis is that she selected R v Coath as an example of violence, or systemic violence as she would have it, on the frontier of the Western Pacific labour trade. On the conviction of John William Coath for kidnapping, her assertion of violence on the frontier would be proved. But Coath can only stand as a single incident of violence because she does not present any other cases of proven violence. She does, of course, mouth off about the leftwing view that colonialism and colonialisation are by definition acts of violence in themselves, but that is a theory put forward by the Black Armband school of thought. The failure of Banivanua-Mar's argument lies in her neglect to read the report on the case of John William Coath by the Attorney-General sent to the Marquis of Normanby, Governor of Queensland dated Crown Law Offices, Brisbane, 24 September 1873, which formed the basis of Coath's pardon. The Attorney-General found that the natives consented to come onboard the vessel and be taken to Queensland as labourers.[232] Therefore, there were no acts of compulsion, abduction or

---

231 Banivanua-Mar, 2005 pp 303, 304, 305, 307 & 308.
232 Maryborough Chronicle, Wide Bay and Burnett Advertiser 29 January 1874 p 4.

kidnapping of the natives, let alone any actual acts of violence against the islanders.

The Black Armband School of Thought approach the historiography of Australian Colonial Settler Studies with a fixed ideological axiom of resistance to invasion. Their articles and publications encourage unity of thought in support of this axiom by stressing and interpreting the historical sources and material in a tendentious and selective manner.

TABLE A - MARINE INCIDENTS

Ship/Port	Date	Location	Event	Remarks
Reliance, Rockhampton	2 Apr 1868	Indispensable Reef	Wrecked, kanakas left on ship	White crew 4 lost; 70 kanakas to rafts, presumed drowned
Spunkie Bowen	April 1868	High Seas	Attempted rape of Tanna girl	Ross Lewin, no case to answer
Prima Donna, Mackay	6 Dec 1868	Valea Island	Boat crew attacked by natives	3 wounded by arrows, unprovoked
Daphne, Bne	Aug 1868	High Seas	Daggett & Pritchard	No case of slavery
Daphne, Bne	Aug 1868	High Seas	Charge of Slaver	NG, V. Adm Crt. Sydney
Active, Sydney	1869	Santa Maria Is.	Delargy charged -kidnapping 7 SSIs	Kidnapping charge withdrawn Bne Police Court
Jason, Maryboro	Feb 1871	High Seas	R v Coath, charge kidnapping 9 SSI.	Guilty 5 yrs jail, Sup Crt. Bne; pardoned 1 Sept 1873
Stormbird, Mackay	18 Apr 1871	Aoba Is. (Ambae)	Boat crew attacked	Recruiting, killed mate, seaman, native
Isabella, Mackay	15 June 1871	Pentecost Is.	Boat crew attacked with spears arrows	Unprovoked 3 crew wounded
Isabella, Mackay	19 & 20 June 1871	Aurora Is. & St. Clair	Boat crew attacked with spears arrows	Unprovoked returned fire on natives
Fanny Campbell, Mackay	18 Mar 1872	Santa Maria Is. (Gaua Is.)	Wrecked on reef ship lost all saved	Wreck plundered by natives
Restless, Brisbane	5 May 1872	Torres Is.	Boats fired on bows & arrows	C Brown G.A. wounded died of lock-jaw
Restless, Brisbane	24 July 1872	North Solitaries	Sprung a leak & foundered	All saved, ship lost
Crishna, Sydney	Jan 1873	Cape Sidmouth	R v Crishna carrying without licence	Ship condemnd & forfeited, V. Adm Crt. Brisbane
Melanie, Sydney	5 Jan 1873	Fitzroy Is.	R v Melanie carrying without licence	Ship condemned & forfeited, V. Adm Crt. Syd

TABLE A

Ship, Port	Date	Location	Event	Outcome
Challenge, Sydney	5 Jan 1873	Fitzroy Is.	R v Challenge carrying without licence	Ship condemned & forfeited V. Adm Crt. Syd
Aurora, Sydney	31 Aug 1873	Solomon Is.	R v Aurora carrying w/o licence	No power to seize cargo, V. Adm Crt.
May Queen, Brisbane	4 Dec 1873	Erromango Is.	R v McKinnon kidnapping	No case, prisoner discharged.
Jessie Kelley, Maryboro	2 Apr 1874	Mallicollo Is.	Recruiting boat crew hit by arrows	Coath died from poison arrow wound
Mary Stewart, Mackay	3 June 1874	Pau-uma Is.	Wrecked, all saved, vessel lost	Marine inquiry held outcome unknown.
Southern Cross, Rockhampton	2 Aug 1874	Torres Is.	Attack on boat crew G.A. & chief officer murdered	Unprovoked without GA ship ordered by RN to return Rockhampton
Margaret and Jane,	27 Aug 1874	Bowen	R v Margaret and Jane carrying w/o licence	Not proceeded with, V. Adm Crt., Brisbane
Mystery Mackay	Oct-Jan 1875	Various Islands	Boats fired on	No injuries or damage
Stanley, Maryboro	13 July 1875	Aoba Is.	Recruiter's boat crew attacked	Unprovoked several crew wounded
Lady Darling, Mackay	13 Oct-Dec 1875	Malaita is.	Boat crew attacked spears & arrows	Unprovoked Capt. Belbin & crew wounded
Lyttona, Mackay	12 Nov 1875	Hada Bay	Wrecked, ship lost	All saved; Capt. exonerated
May Queen, Brisbane	3 Apr 1876	Fatuna Is.	John Slade, G.A. drowned recruiting	Capt. Kilgour returned to Brisbane
Lucy and Adelaide, Townsville	25 Jun 1876	Malo Is.	Capt. Andersen killed by natives	Recovering trade for boy who reneged on contract of labour
Chance, Cardwell	Nov 1877	High Seas	Black crew member assaulted SSI female	At Herbert River, SSI sentenced to 6 mths
May Queen, Brisbane	30 Jul 1878	Erromango Is.	Boat crew attacked	Crew recovered by ship
May Queen, Brisbane	17 Aug 1878	Pentecost Is.	Watering party mate & native murdered	Unprovoked ambushed on shore.

Ship, Port	Date	Location	Incident	Outcome
Sybil, Maryborough	4 Nov 1878	Pentecost Is.	Second officer wounded	Sybil crew aiding HMS Beagle over May Queen
Mystery, Mackay	9 Nov 1878	Aoba Is.	Boat crew of mate & G.A. attacked	Natives kill mate, G.A. & 4 black crew & stole boat
Mystery, Mackay	21 Apr 1879	Aoba Is.	Boat stolen above recovered by Capt.	Capt. convicted by Levuka Crt of destroying native property
Noumea, Mackay	13 May 1880	Saumarez Reef	7 South Sea Islanders drowned	Inquiry held mate cause of wreck
Superior, Mackay	May 1880	Bunkhill Bay	Boat crew fired on	Crew returned fire killing native
Lady Darling, Brisbane	7 Mar 1881	Mallicollo Is.	Wreck on reef by tidal surge	All saved; ship lost
Stormbird, Mackay	7 Apr 1881	Moona Bay	Boat's crew fire on; returned fire	RN investig fined village 10 pigs.
May Queen, Mackay	22 May 1881	Aoba Is.	Boat crew 8 natives + McDonald killed	Boat recruiting unprovoked; RN investig a chief shot
Janet Stewart, Mackay	12 Feb 1882	Malaita Is.	R v Thomas set fire to ship	Nolle entered Sup Court, Maryboro.
Janet Stewart, Mackay	12 Feb 1882	Malaita Is.	Ship attacked and burnt	Murdered: Lochhead G.A.; Mr Penny Mate; O'Brien, cook, Jackson, AB, Petersen, AB & Roberts, AB
Lady Belmont, Mackay	8 Mar 1882	Flat-Top Is.	Driven ashore by a gale, ship lost	All hands saved, including kanakas
Jabberwock, Brisbane	24 May 1882	Santa Maria Is. (Gaua Is.)	Boat crew recruiting	Boats fired on, unprovoked
Magnet, Townsville	17 May 1882	Tanna Is.	Wrecked on reef, crew saved	Wrecked & plundered by natives.
Io, Townsville	6 Aug 1882	Wansfell-Marion Reef	Struck reef, all saved	Recruiting cruise, no SSI onboard

TABLE A

Ship, Port	Date	Location	Incident	Outcome
Chance, Maryborough	16 Aug 1882	Tongoa Is.	Wrecked through missed stays	plundered by natives; all saved, Capt. exonerated
Roderick Dhu, Maryboro	Aug 1882	Pau-uma Is.	Recruits returned to home island	Islanders murder and eat returnees
Roderick Dhu, Maryboro	Aug-Oct 1882	Santa Maria Is.	Recruiting boat crews fired on	unprovoked
Roderick Dhu, Maryboro	13 July 1882	White Cliffs	R v Lynn G.A. man-slaughter	Killing deranged returnee, nolle entered
Pioneer, Dungeness	24 Sept 1882	Rua Sura Is.	Wrecked on reef by gale; ship lost all saved	Marine Inquiry Capt.'s certificate suspended 6 mths, mate suspended for 12 mths
Helena, Bundaberg	Oct 1882	Epi Is.	Recruits returned to home island	3 killed and left on beach, ship's crew bury bodies at sea
Helena, Bundaberg	Oct 1882	Tongoa Is.	Recruiting Tongoa natives board ship	3 Tongoa killed in taking back ship from natives
Lizzie, Brisbane	2 Nov 1882	Tanna Is.	Boat fired on, mate minor wound	Returned to Brisbane with labour
Eliza Mary, Maryboro	12 Dec 1882	Tanna Is.	Boats fired on by natives	Decoyed in, oarsman shot and killed
Roderick Dhu Maryboro	2 Feb 1883	Santa Maria Is.	Boat fired on	No injuries, boat damaged
Stanley, Brisbane	17 Apr 1883	Laughlan Is.	R v McMurdo & Davies kidnapping	Taken to Fiji on warrants, convicted; 3 mths goal
Fanny, Brisbane	11 May 1883	Isle of Man	Boat crew & shore party attacked	Capt. & G.A. wounded, 1 native interpreter killed
Stanley Brisbane	1 July 1883	Indispensable Reef	Wrecked ship lost	All saved; cancelled Capt. certificate of competency

Forest King Brisbane	12 July 1883	Malo Is.	J. Samoa boat crew murdered	Crew buying yams from natives
Borough Belle, Mackay	25 July 1883	Ambrym Is.	Capt. Belbin murdered by natives	Unprovoked, attempted to settle dispute
Lavinia, Mackay	25 Aug 1883	Epi Is.	Boat fired on	G.A. Steedman & Cooper killed + 2 natives
Alfred Vittery Maryboro	4 Oct 1883	High Seas	R v Grimes & others, murder of SSI	Grimes guilty-manslaughter rest NG Sup Crt. Brisbane Discharged on recog.
Alfred Vittery Maryboro	20 Dec 1883	Cape Pitt Solomon Is.	Boats fired on while sounding	unprovoked
Jessie Kelley, Mackay	21 Dec 1883	Matana Is.	R v Spall & Milman kidnapping	NG, Sup Crt. Brisbane
Ceara Brisbane	Dec-Feb 1884	Louisiade Archipelago	Recruited under false pretence	Royal Com-recruits retd home
Lizzie Townsville	Dec-Feb 1884	Mewstone Is.	Recruited under false pretence	Royal Com-recruits retd home
Ceara Townsville	Mar-Apr 1884	Bentley Is.	Recruited under false pretence	Royal Com-recruits retd home
Lizzie Townsville	Mar-June 1884	Moresby Is.	Recruited under false pretence	Royal Com-recruits retd home
Sybil Mackay	Apr-Oct 1884	Santa Anna	Recruited under false pretence	Royal Com-recruits retd home
Hopeful Townsville	May-July 1884	Moresby Is.	Recruited under false pretence	Royal Com-recruits retd home
Forest King Brisbane	May-Oct 1884	Rossel Is.	Recruited under false pretence	Royal Com-recruits retd home

TABLE A

Ship	Date	Location	Charge	Outcome
Heath Mackay	Jul-Nov 1884	Kaan Is. (Tanga)	Recruited under false pretence	Royal Com-recruits retd home
Emily Brisbane	19 Feb -24 Jun 1884	High Seas	Allegations of G.A. misconduct by Capt. McDougall	Inquiry held: Capt. McDougall, Palziard, and Crawford disbarred
Forest King Brisbane	17 Jan 1884	Fisher's Is.	R v McLean & Rowen kidnapping	G, mercy 3 years, first in irons Sup Crt
Alfred Vittery Maryboro	8 Feb 1884	Caen Is. (Tanga)	Wrecked on reef	Saved taken onboard by Lochiel
Forest King Brisbane	9 July 1884	Anchor Is.	R v Owners Kidnapping	Not guilty, ship restored to Owners V-Adm Crt. Brisbane
Ethel, Maryboro	24 Feb 1884	Pau-uma Is.	Natives fired on second boat	Unprovoked, no injuries or damages
Madeline Brisbane	17 Apr 1884	High Seas	Breach of Recruiting Rules	Inquiry Capt disbarred, GA resigned
Ethel, Maryboro	7 July 1884	New Ireland	R v Mills & Burton kidnapping, guilty	Mills-7 yrs jail, Burton-2 yrs jail 1st yr in irons, Sup Crt Bne
Ethel, Maryboro	7 July 1884	New Ireland	R v Loutit, kidnapping	Sup Crt Bne Not Guilty
Hopeful, Townsville	13 Jun 1884	High Seas	R v McNeil murder	Guilty, sentenced to death, Sup Crt Brisbane
Hopeful, Townsville	13 Jun 1884	High Seas	R v Williams murder	Guilty, death, Sup Crt. Bne
Hopeful Townsville	13 Jun 1884	High Seas	R v Shaw, Schofield, Freeman, Rogers, Preston, kidnapping	Guilty: life, 3 yrs in irons; life, 3 yrs in irons; 10 yrs, 2 yrs irons; 7 yrs, 1 yr in irons; 7 yrs, 1 yr in irons; Bne Sup Crt

Vessel	Date	Location	Incident	Outcome
Fredericka Wilhelmina	18 Feb 1884	Hardy's Is.	Roe G.A. recruiting attacked by natives	Wounded taken to Lochiel returned to Mackay
Fredericka Wilhelmina	31 Mar 1884	Fade Island	Wrecked crew, GA & recruits saved	First mate, 2 ABs and native lost at sea
Jabberwock Mackay	23 May 1884	Loake Is.	Wrecked ship lost	Recruiting all saved.
Flora Townsville	Jan-Jun 1884	Santa Maria Is.	Fired on boat crews	RN investig; natives fined 3 rifles 9 pigs
Chinese junk, Mourilyan Harbour	Aug 1884	Murray Island	New Guinea natives steal junk to return home	Agreed to work for 3 months. Returned by RN
Heron, Maryboro	14 Oct 1884	Aneityum Is.	Wrecked on reef by strong gale	All saved, ship lost
Emily, Brisbane	18 Dec 1884	Hogg Harbour	Natives fired on vessel, no injuries	Rannie G.A. destroyed native property-justified.
Madeline Townsville	Nov-Jan 1885	New Hebrides	Natives fired on boat crew 3 times	White crew member wounded
Elibank Castle, Brisbane	15 Jan 1885	Benyetta Is.	Killed Capt. Howie, Johann AB, & 3 native crew	Trader copra & tortoise shell, unprovoked.
Young Dick Maryboro	10 Mar 1885	Mallicollo Is.	Fired on recruiting boats no damage	HMS Undine found work of individual not tribe
Emily Brisbane	28 Mar 1885	Strait of Malo	Wrecked on reef all saved	Recruits carried by Borough Belle
Elibank Castle, Brisbane	17 May 1885	Solomon Is.	Killed Capt. Routch, mate, cook, Richards & a native	Trader copra, 2 boat crew wounded, Brown survived
Douro Melbourne	23 May 1885	High Seas	R v Sorensen assault on C Leslie, G 5 yrs	Trader, Sup Crt Bne, appeal dismissed.

TABLE A

Ship/Port	Date	Location	Incident	Notes
Douro Melbourne	18 Oct 1885	Carpenter Is	R v Sorensen, robbery under arms, G 10 yrs jail	Trader, stealing bêche-de-mer from natives, Sup Crt Bne, appeal refused.
Douro Melbourne			Ship forfeited s103 (2), concealment	Merchant Shipping Act 1854, V-Admty Crt, Bne
Flora Brisbane	Oct 1885	Tanna Is.	Boat crew fired on	Islander killed; white man wounded
Ceara Townsville	17 Nov 1885	Santa Maria Is. (Gaua Is.)	Wrecked, anchor cable parted	Ship lost; all saved by Eliza Mary
Hector Brisbane	15 Feb 1886	Aoba Is.	Disembarked ship because of gale	Aoba natives stole landed stores from the ship
Madeline Brisbane	19 Feb 1886	Malo Pass	Hit reef and run ashore	Recruits taken by Hector; ship and crew saved
Young Dick Brisbane	May 1886	Malaita Is. Cape Zele'e	Hornidge 2nd mate attacked wounded	RN Opal investigated shelled village
Young Dick Brisbane	20 May 1886	Malaita Is.	ship attacked, killed 4 whites, 1 kanaka	Crew defended ship killed 15 or more natives
Young Dick Brisbane	July 1886	High Seas	Lost at sea presumed drown	Over 117 recruits & 3 crew
Sybil Maryboro	14 Aug 1886	Mallicollo Is.	Boat crew fired on; crew returned fire	No harm done to either party
Hector Brisbane	Mar-Aug 1886	San Cristobal Is.	Landed 4 return recruits	Days later 2 killed and eaten
Sybil Maryboro	24 Jan 1887	Southwest Bay, Mallicollo Is.	Wrecked in gale on a reef; 1 returnee & 2 return children lost	Remaining crew and recruits rescued
Forest King Brisbane	Feb 1887	Shortland Is.	Three Malaita returns left the ship	On shore murdered by islanders

Eliza Mary Bundaberg	22 Dec 1887	Over the cruise	Gross behaviour towards G.A.	Inquiry held Master & 1 crew barred from service
Madeline Maryboro	16 Apr 1888	Tongoa Is.	Wrecked by hurricane	All saved hull sold for £10
Ariel Bundaberg	26 Jun 1888	High Seas	Suicide of G.A. Murray	Capt. Lewis held negligent
Hector Mackay	Aug 1888	Port Sandwich	Crew drinking and fighting	Capt. Weston disbarred from labour trade
Helena Bundaberg	22 Oct 1888	Ambrym Is.	Boat crew fired on; return fire made	Mate-Heath, Olsen-AB killed, native wounded
Eliza Mary, Brisbane	12 Nov 1888	Pau-uma Is.	Boat crew ambushed	GA wounded, HMS Opal shelled village
Ariel Bundaberg	6 Dec 1888	Manoba Is.	Killed Armstrong Gov Agent	Recruiting, unprovoked
Northern Belle, Cairns	28 Feb 1889	Motlab (Mota) Is.	Wrecked by gale	4 white + 16 natives lost at sea; ship lost
Borough Belle	12 Feb 1889	Rano Is.	Fired on vessel	RN reported incident
Myrtle Maryboro	1 Mar 1889	High Seas	Wrecked in hurricane	Made Samarai, BNG, vessel condemned; all saved
Eliza Mary Herbert River	29 July 1889	Walla Is.	Fired on vessel	RN reported incident
May Herbert River	Sept 1889	Malotine	Crew destroyed coconut trees	RN reported incident
Eliza Mary Cairns	28 Sept 1889	Nguna Is.	Recruited 2 boys employed by Milne	Results of RN investigation unknown
Eliza Mary Dungeness	6 Mar 1890	Mallicollo Is.	Wrecked 5 whites + 46 recruits lost	Presumed drowned on leaving ship
Lucy And Adelaide	Mar-Apr 1890	Espiegle Bay	Capt. & crew drunk & disorderly	Results of inquiry unknown, Capt. possibly disbarred

Nautilus Brisbane	21 Apr 1890	Ambrym Is.	Recruit ran amuck, was killed	RN investigation, killing justified
May Bundaberg	16 Oct 1890	Mallicollo Is.	Illegal recruiting	RN investig, instructed to return illegal recruits
Roderick Dhu Maryboro	1890	Mallicollo Is.	Recruiting under age boys	RN investig, instructed to return boys
Hector Brisbane	19 Apr 1891	Aoba Is.	Hey Dow SSI shot by G Anderson	Inquiry, accident alleged
Sybil	8 Aug 1891	Malaita Is.	Boats fired on 4 hit 3 white 1 native	RN shelled village
Foam Maryboro	6 Nov 1892	Pau-uma Is.	Ret kanaka shot	Killed for past offence
Foam Maryboro	29 Nov 1892	Mallicollo Is.	Boats fired on	unprovoked returned fire
Foam	9 Feb 1893	Myrmidon Reef	Totally wrecked	SSI saved & re-engaged
Empreza	21 July 1893		Illegal recruiting, expired licence	Recruit free agent, no time limit on licence
Ariel	25 Sept 1893	Tanna Is.	G.A. not in recruiting boat	Capt. failed to act disbarred from service
Roderick Dhu	26 Sept 1893	Espiritu Santo	Fired on by natives, return fire made	No injuries or damage
Ariel Bundaberg	7 Apr 1894	Santa Catalina	Wrecked on a reef	All saved, vessel broke up & lost
William Manson Mackay	24 May 1894	Malaita Is.	R v Vos, Olver, Curry, Hall & Dowsett kidnapping	Not Guilty, Sup Crt, Bne; Capt. & crew disbarred & G.A. sacked
Para, Brisbane	1 Jan 1894	Malaita Is.	Boat crew fired on returned fire	No injuries RN investig; bush tribe cautioned

Sybil	11 July 1894	Qui (Kwi) Is.	Fired on by natives returned fire	RN investig; notified by Qld Governor
Rio Loge Bundaberg	July-Aug 1894	Buka Buka Is.	Ship fired on	Bullet struck the ship's deck
Rio Loge Bundaberg	27 Jan 1896	Malaita Is.	Recruiter Bergin shot & killed	RN investig: recruiter fired first; natives retd fire self-def
Roderick Dhu Maryboro	Oct 1898	Erromango Is.	Fired on boat crew no injuries	RN investig and seized natives' guns
Helena	1899	Ambrym Is.	Fired on boat crew	Fire retd; no harm done
Helena Maryboro	31 July 1899	Hook Point Spit	Wrecked due to weather	Captain A. R. Reynolds severely censured
Fearless Bundaberg	19 Apr 1901	Malaita Is.	Recruiter J. Arthur killed by natives	Body recovered and buried
Roderick Dhu Maryboro	9 Sept-Feb 1902	Malaita Is.	Recruiter G M'Cabe killed by natives	Reported to Resident Tulagi
Fearless Maryboro	31 Jan 1902	San Cristobal Is.	Wrecked on reef	All saved
Ivanhoe Maryboro	1 Mar 1902	Florida Is.	Vessel grounded	Ship abandoned, all saved
Coquette Townsville	5 Dec 1902	Townsville	Caught fire all saved	Ship destroyed

NUMBER OF LABOUR VESSEL TRIPS PER YEAR & PASSENGERS - QUEENSLAND

Year	No.Trips Out/Returns	Returns	No.Trips In/Arrivals	Recruits	Source Reference
1868			8	604	QSA IDITM18833.
1869	5	240	6	312	Statistcs of the Colony of Queensland, 1869. QSA IDITM18834, QSA IDITM18833.
1870	15	597	10	638	Statistics of the Colony of Queensland, 1870. QSA IDITM18834, QSA IDITM18833.
1871	14	750	18	1352	Statistics of the Colony of Queensland, 1871. QSA IDITM18834, QSA IDITM18833.
1872	10	447	7	461	Statistics of the Colony of Queensland, 1872. QSA IDITM18834, QSA IDITM18833.
1873	15	250	14	994	Statistics of the Colony of Queensland, 1873. QSA IDITM18834, QSA IDITM18833.
1874	23	1060	21	1503	Statistics of the Colony of queensland, 1874. QSA IDITM18834, QSA IDITM18833.
1875	33	428	33	2682	Statistics of the Colony of Queensland, 1875, QSA IDITM18834, QSA IDITM18833.
1876	23	645	21	1688	Statistics of the Colony of Queensland, 1876.
1877	21	906	24	1986	Statistics of the Colony of Queensland, 1877.
1878	24	1628	19	1421	Statistics of the Colony of Queensland, 1878.
1879	22	1354	23	2182	Statistics of the Colony of Queensland, 1879.
1880	28	1564	22	1997	Statistics of the Colony of Queensland, 1880.
1881	29	1048	31	2643	Statistics of the Colony of Queensland, 1881.
1882	46	1200	34	3140	Statistics of the Colony of Queensland, 1882.
1883	63	1114	59	5276	Statistics of the Colony of Queensland, 1883.
1884	46	2002	48	3265	Statistics of the Colony of Queensland, 1884.
1885	32	1857	32	1916	Statistics of the Colony of Queensland, 1885.
1886	27	2690	25	1595	Statistics of the Colony of Queensland, 1886.
1887	31	2072	29	1988	Statistics of the Colony of Queensland, 1887.
1888	32	1290	34	2291	Statistics of the Colony of Queensland, 1888.
1889	30	1184	31	2032	Statistics of the Colony of Queensland, 1889.
1890	42	1373	36	2459	Statistics of the Colony of Queensland, 1890.
1891	8	976	15	1050	Statistics of the Colony of Queensland, 1891.
1892	11	829	6	464	Statistics of the Colony of Queensland, 1892.
1893	19	1282	14	1211	Statistics of the Colony of Queensland, 1893.
1894	20	803	22	1859	Statistics of the Colony of Queensland, 1894.
1895	12	743	16	1305	Statistics of the Colony of Queensland, 1895.
1896	11	608	11	782	Statistics of the Colony of Queensland, 1896.
1897	12	884	11	934	Statistics of the Colony of Queensland, 1897. PI Immigration Annual Report 1898
1898	13	693	12	1178	Statistics of the Colony of Queensland, 1898. PI Immigration Annual Report 1899
1899	20	923	16	1522	Statistics of the Colony of Queensland, 1899. PI Immigration Annual Report 1900
1900	20	940	20	1743	Statistics of the Colony of Queensland, 1900. PI Immigration Annual Report 1901
1901	22	873	20	1726	Statistics of the Colony of Queensland, 1901. PI Immigration Annual Report 1902
1902	14	1775	18	119	Statistics of Queensland, 1902. PI Immigration Annual Report 1903
1903	12	1065	12	1038	Statistics of Queensland, 1903. PI Immigration Annual Report 1904
1904	4	635	6	78	Statistics of Queensland, 1904. PI Immigration Annual Report 1905
1905	7	933			Statistics of Queensland, 1905.
1906		2438			Statistics of Queensland, 1906.
1907		3278			Statistics of Queensland, 1907.
Total		45377		59434	

Bibliography

Banivanua-Mar, Tracey, 2005, Consolidating violence and colonial rule: discipline and protection in colonial Queensland, Postcolonial Studies, Vol. 8, No. 3.

Beaule, Christine D., editor, 2017, Violence in Early Maritime Encounters in the Pacific, Frontiers of Colonialism. University Press of Florida.

Bolton, G. C., 1970, A thousand miles away: a history of North Queensland to 1920, Australian National University Press, Canberra.

Coghlan, T. A., 1969, Labour and industry in Australia from the first settlement in 1788 to the establishment of the Commonwealth in 1901, Macmillan of Australia Volume 2, Melbourne.

Corris, Peter, 1970, Pacific Island Labour Migrants in Queensland, The Journal of Pacific History, Vol. 5.

Corris, Peter, 1970, Passage, Port and Plantation A History of Solomon Islands Labour Migration, 1870-1914, Thesis, ANU.

Corris, Peter, 1973, Passage, Port and Plantation: A History of Solomon Islands Labour Migration, 1870-1914, Melbourne University Press.

Davidson, J. W., 1966, Problems of Pacific History, The Journal of Pacific History, Vol. 1 (1966), pp. 5-21.

Davidson, J. W. and Scarr, D., 1970, Pacific Islands Portraits, Australian National University Press, Canberra.

Dillon, Paul, 2022, Bêche-de-mer and the Binghis.

Dillon, Paul, 2023, Dispela Kantri Bilong Mi, Nau! Queensland Annexes New Guinea.

Docker, Edward Wybergh, 1970, The Blackbirders, the Recruiting of South Seas Labour for Queensland, 1863-1907, Angus and Robertson, Sydney.

Engerman, Stanley L., 1893, Contract Labor, Sugar, and Technology in the Nineteenth Century, The Journal of Economic History, Sep., 1983, Vol. 43, No. 3.

Evans, Raymond, Saunders, Kay & Cronin, Kathryn, 1993, Race Relations in Colonial Queensland A History of Exclusion, Exploitation and Extermination, University of Queensland Press, St Lucia.

Grant, A. C., Early Station Life in Queensland, Mitchell Library, NSW.

Griggs, Peter, 2000, Sugar Plantations in Queensland, 1864-1912: Origins, Characteristics, Distribution, and Decline, Agricultural History, Vol. 74, No. 3 (Summer, 2000), pp. 609-647.

Moore, Clive, 1981, Kanaka Maratta: a history of Melanesian Mackay, PhD thesis, James Cook University.

Moore, Clive, 1982, Revising the Revisionists: The Historiography of Immigrant Melanesians in Australia, Pacific Studies, Vol. 15, No. 2.

Moresby, John, 1876, New Guinea & Polynesia. Discoveries & surveys in New Guinea and the D'Entrecasteaux Islands; a cruise in Polynesia and visits to the pearl-shelling stations in Torres Straits of H. M. S. Basilisk, J. Murray, London.

Munro, Doug, 1994, Who 'Owns' Pacific History? Reflections on the Insider/Outsider Dichotomy, The Journal of Pacific History, Dec., Vol. 29, No. 2 (Dec., 1994), pp. 232-237.

Munro, Doug, 1995, The Labor Trade in Melanesians to Queensland: An Historiographic Essay, Journal of Social History, Spring, Vol. 28, No. 3 (Spring, 1995), pp. 609-627.

Munro, Doug, 1995, Revisionism and Its Enemies: Debating the Queensland Labour Trade, The Journal of Pacific History, Vol. 30, No. 2 (Dec., 1995), pp. 240-249.

Nolan, Janette Gay, 1977, A History of Bundaberg, 1840-1920, A thesis submitted to the History Department of the University of Queensland for the degree of Master of Arts, Brisbane.

Palmer, George, 1871, Kidnapping in the South Seas, being a narrative of a three months' cruise of H.M. Ship Rosario, Edmonston, Edenborough.

Parnaby, O. W., 1964, Britain and the labour trade in the southwest Pacific, Duke University Press, Durham, N.C.

Price, Charles A. and Baker Elizabeth, 1976, Origins of Pacific Island Labourers in Queensland, 1863-1904: A Research Note, The Journal of Pacific History, Vol. 11, No. 2, Labour Trade [Part 2] pp. 106-121.

Rannie, Douglas, 1912, My Adventures Among South Sea Cannibals; an account of the experiences and adventures of a government official among the natives of Oceania, Seeley, Service & Co. Limited, London.

Saunders, Kay, 1982, Workers in Bondage The Origins and Bases of Unfree Labour in Queensland 1824-1916, University of Queensland Press St Lucia.

Scarr, Deryck, 1967, Recruits and Recruiters: A Portrait of the Pacific Islands Labour Trade, The Journal of Pacific History, Vol. 2 (1967), pp. 5-24.

Shineberg, Dorothy, 1967, They Came for Sandalwood: A Study of the Sandalwood Trade in the South-West Pacific 1830–1865, Melbourne University Press.

Shineberg, Dorothy 1999, The people trade: Pacific Island Laborers and New Caledonia, 1865-1930, University of Hawai'i: University of Hawai'i Press.

Shlomowitz, Ralph, 1985, Time-Expired Melanesian Labour in Queensland: The Measurement of Job Turnover, 1886-1906, The Journal of Pacific History, Vol. 20, No. 1.

Shlomowitz, Ralph, 1989, Epidemiology and the Pacific Labor Trade, The Journal of Interdisciplinary History, Spring, Vol. 19, No. 4.

Stevens, E. V., 1950, BLACKBIRDING A brief history of the South Sea Islands Labour Traffic and the vessels engaged in it, Historical Society of Queensland, Inc.

Ward, John M, 1948, British Policy in the South Pacific, 1786-1893, Australasian Pub. Co, Sydney.

Wawn, William T; Hay, William Delisle 1893, The South Sea Islanders and the Queensland labour trade, a record of voyages and experiences in the western Pacific, from 1875 to 1891, S. Sonnenschein & co., London.

Windschuttle, Keith, 19 June 2020, Why Australia Had No Slavery: The Islanders, https://quadrant.org.au/opinion/bennelong-papers/2020/06/the-myths-of-south-seas-slavery-in-australia/

Wolfe, Patrick, 2001, Land, Labor, and Difference: Elementary Structures of Race, The American Historical Review, Vol. 106, No. 3 (Jun., 2001), pp. 866-905. https://doi.org/10.2307/2692330 https://www.jstor.org/stable/2692330

Public Record Office, Admiralty records, 1673-1957 [microform] / as filmed by the AJCP.[233]

---

[233] http://nla.gov.au/nla.obj-732027610

Abbreviations

AB	Able seaman
A. & P.	HC, Accounts and Papers, Command Papers
C	Command paper, UK Parliamentary Papers
GA	Government Agent
GG	Queensland Government Gazette
HC	House of Commons
HL	House of Lords Debate
HMS	Her Majesty's Ship
LA	Queensland Legislative Assembly
LC	Queensland Legislative Council
LMS	London Missionary Society
NAA	National Australian Archives
NLA	National Library of Australia
Nolle	Nolle prosequi - discontinuance
PMB	Pacific Manuscripts Bureau catalogue
QSA	Queensland State Archives
RN	Royal Navy
SSI	South Sea Islander
Sup Crt	Supreme Court
TI	Torres Strait Islander
V Admty	Vice Admiralty Court

www.ingramcontent.com/pod-product-compliance
Lightning Source LLC
Chambersburg PA
CBHW052059300426
44117CB00013B/2208